The Coaching Partnership

The Coaching Partnership

Tips for Improving Coach, Mentor, Teacher, and Administrator Effectiveness

Rosemarye T. Taylor and Carol Chanter

ROWMAN & LITTLEFIELD
Lanham • Boulder • New York • London

Published by Rowman & Littlefield
A wholly owned subsidiary of The Rowman & Littlefield Publishing Group, Inc.
4501 Forbes Boulevard, Suite 200, Lanham, Maryland 20706
www.rowman.com

Unit A, Whitacre Mews, 26-34 Stannary Street, London SE11 4AB

British Library Cataloguing in Publication Information Available

Library of Congress Cataloging-in-Publication Data Available
ISBN 978-1-4758-2504-6 (cloth : alk. paper)
ISBN 978-1-4758-2505-3 (pbk. : alk. paper)
ISBN 978-1-4758-2506-0 (electronic)

∞™ The paper used in this publication meets the minimum requirements of American
National Standard for Information Sciences—Permanence of Paper for Printed Library
Materials, ANSI/NISO Z39.48-1992.

Printed in the United States of America

Contents

List of Figures and Tables

FIGURES

TABLES

Preface

Coaching and mentoring are well-known concepts in education. These concepts developed from the work of educators who are resources to ones who have the intention of assisting with the incremental development of another. This development should result in measureable improvement of professional performance. These coaches and mentors are not supervisors but peers who support the self-directed learning of others.

In 1996, Showers and Joyce conceptualized that colleagues would (collaborate to) create instructional plans together, share materials, and would improve in expertise more than if they were isolated and alone in their profession. Fletcher and Mullen (2012) presented coaching as a model that is flexible and not strict in structure with the components of knowing, networking, orienting, and wisdom (KNOW). In many school districts, the coaching concept has developed from an unstructured idea to a more structured process with funded positions that beg for accountability of results for the investment made (Taylor, et al., 2013).

Coaches and mentors have varied roles which are context dependent. For that reason, we use the terms similarly and allow readers to determine the meaning in their own contexts. In this text, coaching and mentoring are sometimes used interchangeably and sometimes differently, with mentors and coaches both having the expectation of reflectively coaching the learner.

Since 2002, accountability has magnified the idea that it takes more than a few administrators to improve student learning outcomes. This realization highlights that teacher leaders are critical to achieving the vision of all students' learning and achieving on Common Core Standards or state standards-based assessments. As teacher leader roles have developed, so have the numbers grown of those who are identified as coaches and mentors. Although some schools have a lone instructional coach or curriculum teacher, other schools have a coach for each grade level or content area taught within the school. The growth in numbers has created the need for *The Coaching Partnership: Tips for Improving Coach, Mentor, and Administrator Effectiveness*, which integrates and clarifies the roles of coaches, mentors, learners, and administrators.

Readers will see examples of how individuals in these roles have essential responsibilities for learners to maximize benefit from the coaching process and for administrators to have impact on the school's overall learning outcomes. Conceptualized as the coaching partnership process, the actions that learners, coaches, mentors, and administrators take either advance the partnership and learner outcomes or retard the coaching partnership process by presenting barriers to continual improvement.

We believe in generative thinking that reflects a growth mind-set. This belief is embodied in professional reflection that leads to action and refinement of professional behaviors. Throughout the text you will see multiple examples of statements and questions for self-reflection or for guiding the reflection of others. Through development of expertise, inquiry, reflection, and commitment, the capacity for continued improvement will be developed. Expected deliverables of our model in *The Coaching Partnership* are improved effectiveness of all in the coaching partnership and improvement in student learning outcomes.

Acknowledgments

Books like this one, *The Coaching Partnership: Tips for Improving Coach, Teacher, and Administrator Effectiveness*, which are written to support the success of teachers and administrators, are not useful without lived examples. The scenarios and examples within this book will seem familiar to you. They represent the challenges and successes of teachers, coaches, mentors, and administrators, like the ones you know. All of those who have crafted, implemented, and benefitted from the concept of instructional coach, mentor, or administrator coach are appreciated by the authors.

Other education leaders have made specific contributions to the authors' learning and are gladly recognized. Without their strategic leadership and development of others, this book would not reflect the reality of learning environments and be of benefit to those who are teaching, coaching, mentoring, and leading in schools. Particular appreciation is extended to the teachers, coaches, mentors, and administrators of Ocoee Middle School and Oak Ridge High School for their collaborative pursuit of excellence and commitment to all learners:

Leigh Ann Bradshaw, Principal, Oak Ridge High School, Orlando, Florida. Connie Goodman, Education Faculty, University of Central Florida, Orlando, Florida. William Gordon, II, Chief Operations Officer, Florida Virtual Schools. Melissa Gray, Administrator, Ocoee Middle School, Ocoee, Florida. Erhan Selcuk Haciomeroglu, Mathematics Faculty, University of Central Florida. Melissa Hancock, Literacy Coach, Oak Ridge High School, Orlando, Florida. Walton John McHale, Principal, Cypress Creek High School, Orlando, Florida. Sam Murfee, Instructional Coach, Oak Ridge High School, Orlando, Florida. Kristin Schomer, Instructional Coach, Millennium Middle School, Sanford, Florida. Mark Shanoff, Principal, Ocoee Middle School, Ocoee, Florida. Lee Ann Spalding, Education Faculty, University of Central Florida, Orlando, Florida.

Chapter 1

Teachers, Coaches, Mentors, and Administrators

Coaching and mentoring are forms of job-embedded professional learning to support an individual's or a group's continual professional effectiveness. Today, coaches and mentors are found in most schools and school districts and represent immense investments of scarce resources. It is predicted for numbers of instructional coaches to increase over the next decade by 300 percent (Edfuel.org, 2014).

As advocates for implementing the positions of coaches and mentors, the authors are concerned that much of the research suggests that implementing coaching and mentoring does not consistently result in improved student learning (Mangin & Dunsmore, 2014; Taylor, et al., 2013). What we have observed is a direct positive relationship between implementation of coaching and mentoring with changes in student learning. Consistently, there have been certain components in place when learning improves: clear roles; expertise in coaching, content knowledge, and pedagogy; self-efficacy grounded beliefs; support by administrators; and a systems approach. These components are discussed with examples in this text.

The Coaching Partnership provides the components needed to success-fully implement the coaching partnership that includes coaches, mentors, teachers, and administrators. In other words, everyone in the partnership is also a learner, although emphasis is on the teacher as learner. Learning is often facilitated by the coach and mentor with knowledgeable support from administrators.

The value of each member of the coaching partnership is equally addressed; thus, this text stands apart from others. The coach, mentor, administrator, and teacher (all who may be learners at one time or another) have active and essential roles in making the partnership productive to improve student learning.

EFFECTIVENESS

The terms "effectiveness" and "effect" relate to professional actions that improve student learning. Within this text, these terms relate to the results of implementation of professional practices. Through research the specific meaning of effectiveness has been refined in contrast to other language like strong, powerful, or quality for which each person may have individual meanings. Teacher effects are the stable relationship between professional actions and improved student performance (Konstantopoulous, 2014). Teacher, coach, mentor, and administrator effectiveness is about the impact their actions have on student learning. A positive effect size is considered at least 0.4 and researchers consider a high-effect size of 0.6 or greater (Hattie, 2009).

Particular expertise is needed to be effective, that is, to improve student learning. Essential expertise includes content knowledge and pedagogical expertise. Together content knowledge and pedagogy make up the professional practice of teaching. Sometimes educators are more confident with either pedagogy or content. It is important to continually improve so that both areas of expertise support student success.

In addition to the expertise needed to be an effective teacher, coaches and mentors need skill in adult communication, relationship building, the coaching process, and reflective practice (Hall & Simeral, 2015). Mentors and coaches have similar roles and require similar expertise to be successful, although both roles may vary by context. As coaches and mentors develop expertise in the identified areas, so will the learners due to modeling and practice experienced within the partnership.

A consistency for teachers, coaches, and mentors is that their success is often enhanced or thwarted by the understanding that administrators have about their roles and how administrators frame coaches' and mentors' roles (Mangin & Dunsmore, 2014; Taylor, et al., 2013; Moxley & Taylor, 2006). The relationships among the administrators, teachers, mentors, and coaches will often determine availability of time for coaching, mentoring, and professional learning.

Administrators determine the value attributed to coaching and mentoring. They also determine how the coaching and mentoring process is communicated within the school and school district. Administrators are second only to teachers in influencing student learning (Louis, et al., 2010). Those who are instructional leaders (focus more on student learning and teaching) are more effective than those who focus on management of the school (Hattie, 2009). For these reasons, we advocate for the administrator to be included in the coaching partnership.

Variations in the coaching and mentoring role with the learner are on a continuum from directive to metacognitive. Figure 1.1 displays the range of

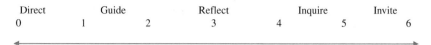

Figure 1.1　Coaching Behavior Continuum from Directive to Metacognitive. *Source*: Rosemarye T. Taylor & Carol Chanter.

coaching and mentoring behaviors to support improved learner effectiveness. Depending upon how the role of coaches and mentors is framed, their behavior will be plotted on the continuum and will guide their practice.

The authors' belief is that like all facilitators of learning, the coach's and the mentor's role and behavior is flexible and should be responsive to the needs of the learner and the context. Over time, the expectation is that coaching and mentoring becomes more reflective and the learner more self-directed, moving to the right and on the continuum. Ultimately the learner invites the coaches' reflection. Roles of those in the partnership are discussed in depth in chapter 2.

SYSTEMATIC APPROACH TO THE COACHING PARTNERSHIP

To have the most improved student learning, systematic processes are essential. This text operationalizes a practical and systematic approach for teachers, coaches, mentors, and administrators to influence each other's effectiveness. All are learners at one point or another in the partnership. Conceptually, coaches, mentors, administrators, and teachers are mutually accountable for student learning and for each other's success. Consistently, evidence-based literature supports the theory that the teacher is the single-most important variable in the learning of students, and professional learning is one factor related to teacher effectiveness (Wenglinsky, 2000). The partnership is a system or systematic process since the components identified work together to create improvement, rather than any one component being sufficient.

SCENARIO: BEGINNING THE PARTNERSHIP

Before the school year began, the principal, Jose Torres, and teacher teams had collaborated to select five new faculty members. Each of the new faculty members had been assigned a mentor who had the same responsibility for students' learning as that of the new teacher. The instructional coach, Mario, had the responsibility of facilitating all new teachers' success during the first semester, which meant collaborating with mentors also.

Principal Torres was relieved that the teacher selection process had gone smoothly. He thought that his part of the process was complete once the five teachers were hired and assigned a mentor. Torres was confident that Mario would show the teachers how to plan standards-based instruction and to understand the instructional expectations in the school.

Mentors were happy to be assigned a learner (teacher) because they knew that a financial bonus was in store for them at the end of each semester as a result of taking on extra responsibility. One of the mentors, Mary, set a regular end-of-the-day sharing time with her learner. Another mentor, Jamal, decided that the best approach was to meet every Friday to be sure standards-based instructional plans were in order for the next week. Two other mentors, Kellie and Josh, thought that the learners (new teachers) would be overwhelmed with the first year in their school and told them to send an e-mail when and if they had questions or needed help. The fifth mentor, Rita, had participated in a mentor preparation workshop and offered to collaboratively develop instructional plans for teaching the standards with her new teacher (learner) and also expressed excitement to learn new instructional strategies from the recent university graduate.

As an instructional coach, Mario was well prepared with a master's degree in teacher leadership, and he also participated in the school district professional learning activities for instructional coaches. Before the first day of school, Mario facilitated a one-day partnership session for mentors and learners to meet, share expectations, and plan their partnerships. Furthermore, he offered to meet with the mentors and new teachers anytime that they needed assistance. Mario's goal was for the new teachers to have maximum opportunities for success and return the following year to teach in the school.

As you reflect on this scenario, which actions by the administrator, mentors, and coach do you think will result in improved student learning?

Which actions do you believe may not result in improved student learning?

Based on the brief scenario, where on the continuum in Figure 1.1 would you place the instructional coach and each mentor? What else do you need to know to place them on the continuum?

How would you coach each of the learners in this partnership scenario?

- Administrator: Principal Torres
- Mentor: Mary, Kellie, Josh, Jamal, Rita
- Coach: Mario

As you continue to read the Tips for Learner, Mentor and Coach, and Administrator, you may want to think again about the scenario and the actions you would take or recommend that another take.

TIPS FOR A PRODUCTIVE PARTNERSHIP

As in the chapters that follow, tips are shared for a productive coaching partnership organized by learner, coach and mentor, and administrator. In this chapter, tips are identified within each of the three partner sections for the learning environment, content, curriculum, pedagogy, and student engagement. This text does not address content- or grade-specific coaching partnerships. With this in mind, and the expectations of content and pedagogical expertise, all in the partnership are encouraged to visit the professional websites of the content area targeted to access resources specific to your goals. A list of the websites is provided in the Resources section at the end of this chapter.

Learner

For teachers to be effective, specific areas of knowledge and skill are needed. The five areas that are essential to the teacher's role are learning environment, content, curriculum, pedagogy, and student engagement. As the target learner in the partnership, there are responsibilities to consider and expertise to gain. The Appendix: Coaching System Planning Tool has a column for Learner Action that may help you generate the steps that you want to take in each area.

Learning Environment

One of the first steps is to establish a learning environment in which each student has a sense of belonging and importance. It is a good idea to plan for and practice with students the routines that you expect for the safety and respect of others in the classroom. Physical examples include how students enter the room, where they put their book bags, digital devices, and coats, and how they move around the classroom. Safety extends to emotional well-being and psychological safety as well. When a classroom is free of put-downs and negative messages from others, a student is more poised to learn than if he or she is fearful of how a comment might be received.

You have the role of establishing the learning environment that is conducive to develop respect among the students and between the students and you. It is common for novice teachers to have some challenges with establishing consistent routines and managing time. Think about asking your mentor and coach if you can observe their classroom to see their organization in action. Conversely, invite them to visit your classroom to help you see through their eyes the structures that are working well or those that may need enhancement.

Content Knowledge

Even with a well-developed environment for learning, students may not make the learning gains that would be expected. Think about the depth of your knowledge of the content standards you are expected to teach. Do you know the content well enough that you can focus on effective instruction or do you have to study the content itself to feel prepared? Students tend to have misconceptions that they learned from both school and personal experiences about science, mathematics, social studies, and writing. Deep content knowledge is essential for teachers to uncover misconceptions, correct misconceptions, and to be sure that misconceptions are not reinforced.

Recent data from first year teachers who had content degrees before learning pedagogy revealed, "I think what has made our classrooms special has been the content knowledge" and "I know ways to relate and make the content relevant and to incorporate real world experience. I think that goes a long way" (Osmond, 2015). Teachers, who do not have deep content knowledge, were heard to say things like, "I stay one chapter ahead of my students." Teachers who are dependent upon the text and teacher guide are not as effective as those empowered with the confidence of deep knowledge.

Ask the coach or mentor and administrator for opportunities to develop content-specific knowledge. As an example, mathematical concepts are often the focus of professional learning for elementary teachers, special education teachers, and English for speakers of other language teachers, since their preparation has historically been more about the students served than about the mathematical concepts themselves. If the mentor has deep content knowledge, ask if you can plan together and ask questions to build confidence in the content.

Curriculum

Standards-based curriculum is expected to be taught to prepare students to be college and career-ready, regardless of the grade level or target content. These standards can be written in ways that are complex and challenging to understand. Following is a typical language arts standard for ninth grade:

> The student can analyze the development of a theme or central idea over the course of a text, including how it emerges and is shaped and refined by specific details and provide an objective summary of the text.

Within this standard are at least four learning goals and tasks for the students. Review the learning goals following this paragraph that reflect an order of instruction. Note that the order starts with summarize and ends with analysis. Analyze is the most rigorous verb in the standard, and students' learning is to be scaffolded to that thinking level through a logical sequence of instruction.

Students will summarize the text to check for understanding and clarity before addressing the theme. Summary is retelling and is at the thinking level of comprehension. Then, the teacher will introduce the theme or central idea, which is abstract rather than concrete. To make the theme concrete, the teacher will connect the concept of the theme by modeling and creating a shared understanding of the identification of the theme in this specific text.

Next, students will be supported as they identify textual evidence and details that support the development of the theme, with the learning task of completing a theme-development graphic organizer. Last, with the graphic organizer as an outline that includes supporting textual evidence, students will communicate in writing and orally how the theme developed over the course of the text.

- Summarize the text.
- Identify the theme or central idea.
- Find textual evidence and details of the theme's development.
- Communicate in writing and orally the analysis of how the theme developed through the text, supported by evidence from the text.

Ask for support in deconstructing the target standards into manageable chunks for instructional planning. Experienced and novice teachers alike find that collaboration to understand standards and plan for student mastery of the standards is helpful.

Pedagogy

Expertise with content and understanding the standards-based curriculum are essential. From the example used in deconstructing the language arts standard, you can see that the pedagogy is linked directly to the standard.

Think about the kind of instruction or pedagogy that teachers used when you learned difficult content and the teachers made it seem easy. These teachers probably used pedagogy that has a high probability of having positive student learning outcomes. You may have heard these strategies, called high-effect size strategies or high-impact strategies (Hattie, 2009, 2012).

Another first year teacher shared his thoughts about content expertise versus pedagogy: "For high achievers my content knowledge is really interesting and engaging but without the pedagogy experience I wouldn't be able to provide for them what I did" (Osmond, 2015). Keep in mind that effective teachers have expertise in their content and in pedagogy.

As a learner, it is your responsibility to identify if you need assistance with high-effect size strategy selection and implementation. Ask mentors and coaches which strategies work best in your content area for specific purposes and if you can observe implementation in their classes. You may want to ask your coach and mentor to arrange for participation in a webinar or book study on such resources as John Hattie's *Visible Learning for Teachers: Maximizing Impact on Learning* (2012) or *Leading, Teaching, Learning the Common Core Standards* (Taylor, et al., 2014).

Engagement

Recently, a frustrated teacher exclaimed, "I know I need to make learning fun and it is exhausting to try to make all instruction fun!" Misconceptions related to student engagement abound. Engagement may be characterized as fun or hands-on, but these two characteristics are misconceptions related to student engagement and improved learning.

Engagement to improve learning means cognitive engagement or engaging students' thinking. On the other hand, students can be cognitively engaged and learn unimportant content, concepts, and skills. Standards-based instruction that engages students intellectually will improve student learning outcomes. Learning tasks that expect thinking at moderate to high levels motivate all learners, adult and children alike. Expectations of rigorous thinking send a message that you believe students are capable and can achieve. Students get bored with low-level thinking and recall thinking-level learning expectations. As a learner, you have the responsibility to find ways of engaging students' thinking about the content, concepts, or skills that are identified in the standards to be learned.

Invite your mentors and coaches to share with you learning tasks and strategies that include thinking and inquiry that they have found to work well. How do they frame open-ended questions, rather than using questions that can be answered with yes or no? Ask, "Will you review the teacher's guide with me to select the most engaging instructional strategies and student learning tasks?"

Coach and Mentor

As coaches and mentors, you support the learner's development of expertise. An important role you play is to ascertain which of the five essential areas for effectiveness should be addressed first. If you have a social studies, science, or mathematics teacher with a degree in the content area, then most likely the learning environment or pedagogy may be the first priority. Conversely, if the teacher does not have a background in standards-based instruction, it will be essential to co-plan instruction to assure understanding of the standard and instructional planning to the rigor of the standard. Review Appendix A Coaching System Planning Tool and identify actions that you will take in the five essential components.

Learning Environment

Offer to assist the learner in designing the learning environment on a device or a sheet of paper. Help them sketch out placement of desks or tables, technology resources, learning centers, classroom libraries, and pathways for student movement. Ask the learner if he or she will be able to have physical proximity with all students to provide instructional support and research-based feedback. Ask, "How will you develop a classroom environment in which all learners are respected and are assured opportunities to learn?"

Content

Learners like to have coaches and mentors who know the same content deeply that they are teaching. Over and over again, when feedback from teachers is reviewed, it is clear that general coaching is not enough. They want support for the specific content they are to teach and for the students' developmental stage, "I want my mentor to provide examples of how she teaches the physics standards" or "Examples of implementing inquiry with primary age children is what I want to see. Do you realize how young they are?"

Curriculum

Find standards-based curriculum-aligned resources and sample instructional plans for teachers if you have not taught the specific curriculum of the learner. School districts, departments of education, and professional organizations have resources related to specific standards-based curriculum. You can expect resources to be available, particularly for the standards that are measured on assessments.

Review the standards to be learned by students and deconstruct them with learners. Invite those who teach the same standards to collaborate on understanding the standards and sequencing the order of the standard segments in a way that makes sense, particularly beginning with the lower level of thinking and scaffolding students to the highest level of rigor within the standard. The highest level of rigor within the standard is the target for student performance.

Pedagogy

Always be a model of research-based pedagogy. None can teach or coach something that he or she does not own. Adopt academic language as described in chapter 5 so that you are always modeling and teaching pedagogy that is expected, and that will result in improved student learning in the learners' content area.

Think about ways to support understanding and owning of research-based pedagogy. Would it be useful to create book studies with texts such as *Visible Learning* (Hattie, 2009), *Visible Teaching* (Hattie, 2012), or *Leading Teaching, Learning the Common Core Standards* (Taylor, et al., 2014)? Teachers and administrators find these books to be accessible, so help them to replace ineffective practices with those that improve learning. Perhaps you will facilitate participation in a webinar and follow with reflection among the members of the group? Keep in mind that as you work with groups, rather than individuals only, your influence on student learning is greater.

Student Engagement

As you collaborate, be clear in how student engagement is framed. Address misconceptions of fun or group activities as important and replace these kinds of activities with standards-based high-effect size strategies and learning tasks. Emphasize that engagement is in students' heads. Engagement takes place when learning tasks invite students to think and apply their learning in both familiar and unfamiliar ways. Analysis should follow to draw conclusions.

Collaborative learning when students are in pairs or triads can also be engaging. Be sure that each student has a specific responsibility. Just asking students to work together without a clear purpose and deliberate actions does not meet the criteria of engagement. As an example, students' learning measurement may have stations in which they measure each other's height and weight to develop proportion or mathematical ratios. In this example, fractions, ratios, proportion, and measurement are learned more deeply through purposeful and deliberate collaboration that requires thinking at the application and analysis levels.

Administrator

Administrators are essential for mutual improvement in effectiveness and to build the culture of coaching. Coaching and mentoring are dependent upon the administrator's understanding and actions. Review with your coaches the resources that provide guidance, such as *Literacy Coaching: A Handbook for School Leaders* (Moxley & Taylor, 2006) or *Mathematics Coaching: Resources and Tools for Coaches and Leaders, K–12* (Bay-Williams & McGatha, 2014) and take steps necessary to leverage the coaching investment. View the INVEST video series with your coaches and mentors, followed by a planning session.

Only as an active participant in the partnership will student learning improvement be maximized. Reflect on the Administrator Action column in Appendix A Coaching System Planning Tool to determine your next steps. Use the tool to support the development of your school culture around coaching and collaboration.

Learning Environment

When you visit classes do you note if the learning environment is one of compliance or engagement? Are the routines clear and do students have what they need to accomplish the learning task? Are there procedures for students to get assistance when needed and to support other students' learning?

Content

Content expertise is essential. Be sure that you know the content well enough to determine if the content is being represented accurately. One way to support your confidence in the content is to ask a content expert from your local university, education organization, school district, or school to visit classes with you and reflect with you. Showcase teachers who regularly and explicitly uncover students' misconceptions and who clarify, model, and demonstrate the difference between misconceptions and accurate understanding.

Curriculum

Instructional plans that extend over a unit will show more standards-based planning than individual lesson plans. Longer-term instructional plans, rather than individual lessons, will help teachers focus on the intended learning outcomes and link day-by-day learning together to scaffold to the rigor of the target standards.

As you visit classrooms, view through the lens of the student. Are the learning tasks worth doing or are they low-level thinking and recall? Do students demonstrate behaviors that indicate wrestling with understanding and celebration when understanding occurs?

Pedagogy

Provide professional learning for everyone to clarify research-based pedagogy so that ineffective practice is diminished. In classrooms, listen for accurate use of academic language by students and teachers. Watch for learning tasks at the level of rigor of the target standard. Look for high-effect size instructional strategies and professional practices. Determine the extent to which student learning is scaffolded by the teacher from high support to purposeful and deliberate collaborative learning with moderate support to independent demonstration of mastery with low support (Taylor, et al., 2014).

Engagement

One of the indicators of student engagement is that when asked, students can share their learning task, why they are doing the task, and if they are completing the task with accuracy. When you are in classrooms, speak with students.

- "Tell me what you are doing."
- "How do you know your work is correct?"
- "What happens when you do not understand?"

Examine the classroom culture. Does a learning culture exist that invites students to think, ask questions, and problem-solve? Look for a direct relationship among the target standard and its rigor, the learning task, student engagement, and evidence of student learning.

REFLECTIVE PRACTICE

Metacognition or thinking about one's own learning puts the individual in control and not someone else. Adults thrive when they have control over their environment—whether in their personal or professional lives. When professionals reflect, they think about how specific strategies or projects are working and about the contributions, professional behaviors, or actions that lead to more success or less success. In this section of each chapter, you will be encouraged to reflect on matters related to the chapter's target concepts for the learner, coach and mentor, and administrator.

You may want to access *Teach, Reflect, Learn* (Hall & Simeral, 2015) for a deeper understanding of reflective practice to improve your effectiveness. The intent is for each person in the learning partnership to be empowered to improve the outcomes of the partnership.

Get into the habit of taking a few minutes at the end of each day to think about the day and to celebrate what went well. Make a note of anything you will do differently when you are in a similar situation. Turn to Appendix A, Coaching System Planning Tool, and reflect on the rows and columns that best align with your work.

Learner

In the coaching partnership system, the learner has equal responsibility for the relationship and outcomes. Reflective practice can be an excellent way for you to think about enhancing the partnership to assure your success. Think about the queries that follow and jot down important thoughts.

- When I am unsure of what to do, how do I seek mentoring and coaching?
- How can I ask to be in a coaching and mentoring partnership?
- What should I have handy when I have time with my mentor or coach?

Coach and Mentor

Coaches and mentors generally take the most responsibility for the partnership. In contrast, all in the coaching partnership are equally responsible. Check out the free INVEST video series—*Building a Culture of Coaching and Building a Culture of Collaboration* (http://www.lipscomb.edu/ayers/invest). For specific content coaching, check out organizational websites like Inside Mathematics (http://insidemathematics.org) that have videos to use as examples with teachers and for you to practice your coaching knowledge and skill in mathematics. Think about ways of supporting the learner in actively participating and in taking ownership. Review the reflective items that follow and generate your own.

- How can I let the administrator know what we need?
- What can I do to encourage the learner to ask me for support?
- What are some examples of when and how I model for learners?
- Think about saying, "Before leaving our partnership session, let's set a time for the next one."
- Think about saying, "I learn from you, so let's meet regularly."

Administrator

Analyze your own expertise related to the five components of effective teaching described in the chapter. Seek professional learning and coaching on the ones you believe will help you to be a more effective as a school leader. Review classroom observation videos in specific content areas with your coaches and learn to be specific in providing feedback related to the target content. For mathematics, Inside Mathematics (http://www.insidemathematics.org) has numerous resources for you and your coaches to build expertise in mathematics leading and coaching. Reflect on your role in the partnership and how you can be sure it improves.

- How do I provide time and resources for mentors, coaches, and learners to collaborate for mutual improvement of student learning?
- Ask others, "How can I support, but not direct the partnership?"

BOOK AND CHAPTER ORGANIZATION

This first chapter is the backdrop for coaching and mentoring to be viewed through the lens of a learning partnership in which each participant has an important and equal role, with expectations for making contributions to each other's success. Chapter 2 focuses on role differentiation of each in the partnership. Generative thinking and inquiry as a way of framing coaching is shared in chapter 3. Trust and positive collaborative relationships define the depth of the partnership in chapter 4. Successful professionals are experts in adult communication strategies, which are developed in chapter 5, along with the value of academic language. The coaching process and delivery modes are shared in chapter 6. Chapter 7 provides thoughts on being expert practitioners and high-effect professional behaviors. The final chapter invites commitment to effective systems for coaching, mentoring, learning, and leading.

Readers can follow the predictable organization of each chapter. The focus concepts are presented first. Read with assurance that the concepts are grounded in research, although presented for practical application. To help transfer concepts to your professional practice, scenarios from schools and school districts are included that may help you visualize actions to take and actions to avoid! A section is dedicated to actions for each to take in the partnership: coach and mentor, learner, and administrator. Reflective practice is modeled as you are invited to reflect, before moving to the definitions that support the chapter. Resources for you to consider are included at the end of the chapter and also after Appendix A.

DEFINITIONS

Accountability	Mutual investment in another's success
Administrator	Principal, assistant principal, or supervisor of others
Coach	Teacher leader who has the responsibility to promote improvement in teacher effectiveness and student learning
Effectiveness	Relates to the improvement in student learning
Effect size	Statistical measure that indicates the probability that a particular strategy will improve learning (Taylor, Watson, & Nutta, 2014: Hattie, 2009)
Mentor	Teacher leader who supports the improved effectiveness of another and who uses coaching processes
Learner	Anyone who has a mentor or coach, or is in the learning partnership

RESOURCES

Professional Organizations

International Literacy Association, formerly International Reading Association
National Association of Elementary School Principals
National Association of Secondary School Principals
National Council for the Social Studies
National Council of Teachers of Mathematics
National Council of Teachers of English
National Middle School Association
National Science Teachers Association

Other Resources

Bay-Williams, J. M. & Mc Gatha, M. (2014). *Mathematics Coaching: Resources and Tools for Coaches and Leaders, K–12.* New York: Pearson.

Hall, P. & Simeral, A. (2015). *Teach, Reflect, Learn: Building Your Capacity for Success in the Classroom.* Alexandria, VA: ASCD.

Hattie, J. (2012). *Visible Learning for Teachers: Maximizing Impact on Learning.* New York: Routledge.

Hattie, J. (2009). *Visible Learning: A Synthesis of over 800 Meta-Analysis Relating to Achievement.* New York: Routledge.

http://www.insidemathematics.org.

http://www.lipscomb.edu/ayers/invest (INVEST Video Library).

Konstantopoulous, S. (2014). Teacher effects, value added models, and accountability. *Teachers College Record, 116*: 1–21.

Moxley, D. E. & Taylor, R. T. (2006). *Literacy Coaching: A Handbook for School Leaders.* Thousand Oaks, CA: Corwin Press.

Taylor, R. T., Watson, R., & Nutta, J. (2014). *Leading, Teaching, Learning the Common Core Standards: Rigorous Expectations for All Students.* Lanham, MD: Rowman & Littlefield.

Chapter 2

Roles

Within a coaching partnership there are varied roles for learners, coaches, mentors, and administrators. Clearly defined and well-understood roles will improve collaboration and reduce time wasted on role negotiation (Erickson, 2012).

This chapter begins by exploring the coaching partnership roles for the coach and mentor, learner, and administrator. A scenario example in the practice of education follows. Next, are tips followed by opportunities for reflective practice. Definitions of academic language and resources that may provide additional support for determining roles for productive coaching partnerships complete the chapter.

COACHING PARTNERSHIP ROLES

Though most educators are familiar with some type of instructional coaching, various understandings of coaching roles exist. School coach, school district coach, content coach (e.g., mathematics), data coach, and external coach are but a few of the titles used in school districts. Authors and organizations have explained the role of coach by focusing on the purpose of the role. As an example, the International Literacy Association (ILA) (2004) issued a position statement on the roles and responsibilities of literacy or reading coaches. The ILA statement indicates that the primary role is to provide support to teachers in instruction. From this perspective, coaches must be excellent classroom teachers. Other examples of coaching purposes include:

- developing collaborative relationships,
- promoting reflection,
- providing feedback,
- observing instruction,
- participating in leadership meetings,
- gathering and analyzing data,
- supporting curriculum and program implementations,
- providing resources,
- delivering professional learning, (including modeling lessons, co-planning, co-teaching), and
- supporting new teachers (Lyons & Pinnell, 2001; Dole & Donaldson, 2006; Borman, et al., 2006; Walpole & Blamey, 2008).

Even across these experts, the coaching and mentoring role is not consistently defined. All agree that a careful defining of roles and expectations is a necessary step in leveraging coaching to improve teaching effectiveness and student achievement.

Considering the importance of creating clear role definitions, schools and school district leaders are encouraged to dedicate time and effort to the task. Roles should be constructed around the unique structural and instructional goals and influences distinctive to each school district or school (Symonds, 2003). Also, the concepts of instructional leadership and adult learning, as noted in chapter 1 (Annenberg Institute), should be considered.

It will take time to develop, communicate, and fulfill all of the roles within the coaching partnership. Dramatic change within the first year of implementation is rare. It takes time for everyone to adopt, adapt, and succeed in the role.

As roles evolve, partners should examine student work, data, and evidence of student learning to monitor progress and refine roles. With clear roles, measurable and achievable goals, and consistent support, coaching partnership systems will positively impact student achievement.

PARTNERSHIP PRIORITY

Having a well-thought-out focus for coaching can help target and achieve the desired outcomes. When administrators examine and prioritize structural elements, it helps focus coaching. Structural elements include school and school district initiatives, target student populations, achievement, and measures of effectiveness. Without prioritization of these elements, a coach or mentor might try to support all initiatives, content areas, grade levels, and student populations equally.

Without a focus the result will be frustration with little or no measureable change in student learning. In fact, in a recent study, coaches shared their frustration with having clear role expectations but being pulled to attend to other important school-related tasks. These coaches actually spent little time in their well-defined coaching roles (Taylor, et al., 2013).

As you might imagine, when asked to share evidence of their coaching impact, they were challenged to identify any evidence. Typically, they pointed to workshops given or where they spent their time (hall duty, bus duty) but rarely were able to provide evidence of improved student learning or teacher effectiveness.

Administrators define the coaching partnership priority by collaboratively exploring questions to reveal specific structural elements and narrowing priorities. Such coaching partnership questions include the following ones.

- What is the content priority (literacy, writing, mathematics, and other content areas)?
- What is the target student population (English learners [ELs], special education, general education, grade level)?
- What are the target initiatives and the priority levels?
- How will teacher, coach, mentor, and administrator effectiveness be measured (progress monitoring, formative assessment, surveys, summative assessment, student work)?
- How much of each member's time will the partnership take?
- When will partnership experiences take place?

After exploring these questions, one elementary school coaching partnership decided to prioritize the focus on text-dependent questions. A middle school partnership focused on ELs' accurate use of academic language in all content areas. One team of school district leaders decided that those in the partnership would prioritize reasoned argument writing strategies in English language arts and social studies instruction. Readers may find *Taking the Lead: New Roles for Teachers and School-based Coaches* (Killion & Harrions, 2006) to be a helpful resource for examining expectations that may influence the partnership priorities.

PARTNERSHIP ROLE DESCRIPTIONS

Learner Role

The most critical aspect of the learner's role in the coaching partnership is that of equality. For the coaching partnership to be productive, the learner must take on an active, rather than passive role and engage as an equal partner with the coach and mentor.

Learners can take cues from business coaching in which coaches are encouraged to have certain expectations and understandings of the coaching process. Their understandings include priority, delivery format, benefits, approach, timeframe, time commitment, documentation process, communication protocol, and intended outcomes (Alliance Coaching Limited, n.d.; Estrela, 2013). Ask for clarity on any aspect of the partnership that is unknown or vague. Knowing the expectations for you and for the coach or mentor is fundamental to a productive experience.

It is also helpful for learners to reflect on certain questions before, during, and after the coaching or mentoring session to maximize benefit from the experience. Review the following three questions to guide your reflection.

1. As a learner, what do I bring to the partnership?
2. What questions do I still have about the partnership?
3. What outcomes do I hope to gain from the partnership?

To answer the first question, learners bring a deep understanding of their professional needs, student evidence-based needs, professional interests, specific instructional skills, and personal circumstances. Only learners have this information, so it is vital to share these insights with the coach, so the coach can craft the best approach to meet the learner's needs.

To answer the second question, learners may think about and write down any remaining questions they have about the coaching partnership and how it will function. Include questions related to time, communication, documentation, etc. The coaching process addresses many of these elements and will be discussed further in chapter 6.

To answer the third question, learners should tell the coach in clear concise terms about their goal. For example, a learner may say to the coach, "I want to learn more ways to engage students to actively participate in my lessons" or "I want to increase the number of target vocabulary words my English learners use in discussion" or "I want to increase the end of unit test scores by 10 percent." As an equal partner, knowing and stating the goal is an essential step.

Learners may find that completing a coaching request form and survey helps clarify their role and expectations. Examples can be found at the Literacy Coaching Clearing House website and are referenced at the end of this chapter. By participating as an equal, active, willing, and committed partner, learners are more likely to be motivated and committed to achieving the positive change identified as important.

Coach and Mentor Role

Coaching and mentoring are different from traditional professional learning formats. The coaching partnership is considered job-embedded professional learning that takes place in the learning environment. Coaching and mentoring are change agent roles and carry great responsibility.

As introduced in chapter 1, depending on the purpose, coaching roles can range on a continuum from most directive to collaborative and least directive. Generally, the role is thought of as collaborative and as such should invoke inquiry and reflection. Coaching builds on the strengths of those in the partnership. Rather than evaluative, coaching is focused on continuous improvement.

Collaborative coaching and mentoring relationships tend to be longer in duration than more directive coaching and mentoring relationships. More directive coaches may be employed in nonprofit or for-profit organizations for the specific purpose of implementing a new initiative within a certain time frame. The collaborative approach stresses equal contributions of those in the coaching partnership—the coach, mentor, learner, and administrator.

Depending upon the priority and responsibility, some coaches or mentors may have more directive roles than others. As an example, an external coach from a private provider may have been asked to provide direct feedback and next steps to a learner (teacher, coach, mentor, administrator). In this type of coaching model, the school-based coach and mentor may be responsible for following up with the learner and holding the learner accountable for taking the identified next steps. When in a directive role, the coach may even report to the learner's supervisor. Keep in mind that the learner may be an administrator, coach, or mentor and is not always a classroom teacher.

The role of the external coach is different from that of the colleague coach and mentor who is in a similar position to the learner who is being coached. In most school districts, coaches and mentors are teacher-level personnel who do not have authority over another teacher. Probably the peer coach and mentor are neither evaluative nor directive. The same would apply to a principal coach or mentor and one who coaches the school's coach or mentor. With that in mind, coaching roles that are grounded in the day-in and day-out relationship are extremely important.

In defining the role of coach and mentor, the two terms may be interchangeable or may be implemented differently, depending upon the structure and context of the school. As one school coach explained, "As the coach I help with general instructional strategies across all of the teachers. The mentors have expertise in the standards and curriculum of the learner and help with specific instructional planning. For instance the mentor in science helps the learner find lab resources and helps to set up labs."

Just as the degree of coaching directedness moves on a continuum, so do learners' skills. The more learners advance in their careers, the more individualized coaching must become. For example, novice teachers need different kinds of support than those with a consistent history of effectiveness. Likewise, teachers who enter the profession with content degrees but no pedagogical preparation need different types of support. Coaching roles adjust to meet the differentiated needs of learners.

The coaching role is also shaped by how the coach spends his or her work time. Participating in meetings, providing resources, and delivering professional learning are all important aspects of the coaching role. However, if these activities are not carefully managed, they may fragment time and dilute positive change that might otherwise be gained from individual or group coaching.

Coaches must work collaboratively with administrators to focus their work time. The priorities are developing collaborative relationships, co-planning, modeling, and co-teaching. Observing instruction, providing feedback, and facilitating reflection are also important.

At the Florida Literacy Coach Institute in 2015, one of the coaches announced that her administrator protected her from noncoaching duties. The administrator protected her from requests to take on noncoaching responsibilities that absorb time.

Coaches and mentors also carve out time to improve their own practice. By continuously improving mastery of content and pedagogy, the trust and respect of the learners can be earned (Neufeld & Roper, 2003). Some methods for continuous improvement include participating in book studies, webinars, online courses, networking, and social media.

Coaches and mentors may find the following blogs useful as resources to connect, collaborate, reflect, and improve practice.

- The Art of Coaching Teachers, *Education Weekly* blog by Elena Aguilar http://blogs.edweek.org/teachers/coaching_teachers/
- Student-Centered Coaching blog by Diane Sweeney http://dianesweeney.com/student-centered-coaching-blog/

Before exploring the role of the learner, think about the following statements regarding the coach and mentor role. Jot down which you agree with and why. What would you like to add to your role?

- Help learners reflect on what has and has not worked to improve student learning outcomes.
- Help learners identify areas of instructional expertise.

- Help learners set goals and reach them.
- Help learners gather and analyze student evidence of their effective instructional practice.
- Provide models of target instructional behaviors.
- Reflect with the learner.

Coaches and mentors may find that completion of a self-assessment is beneficial when thinking about and refining roles. Examples can be found at the Literacy Coaching Clearinghouse website (http://www.literacycoachingonline.org) and are also referenced at the end of this chapter.

Administrator Role

Administrators differ in perspectives on their role in the coaching process. Some want to be involved daily in the partnership and others trust the coach to handle the work with periodic check-ins. The Annenberg Institute (n.d.) identified instructional leadership as a key component of effective coaching systems. Given that coaches do not have authority to establish wide-reaching expectations, the administrator has a critical role in establishing conditions for success. The coach simply cannot be effective without the regular involvement and support of administrators.

One of the first actions to support the coaching process is to take an active role in establishing a rationale, common understanding, and vision for the coaching partnership. Begin by communicating that the coach is not a supervisor or evaluator.

As suggested by Taylor, Moxley, Chanter, and Boulware (2007), teachers tend to be suspicious of those in nonteaching positions. To overcome distrust and maximize learning gains, the administrator will carefully develop the role of coach and mentor by prioritizing all professional learning. The coach, mentor, and faculty need to understand expectations, why coaching and mentoring are important, and how assistance will be provided. Their role as learners in the partnership should be understood.

Establishing a practice of celebrations for learner accomplishments and milestone achievement can help earn learners' trust. As a former principal, the author Carol posted positive notes during after-school walkthroughs celebrating evidence of coaching action steps. Such notes highlighted and reinforced new instructional strategies. Evidence of implementation of professional learning was recognized.

This leadership practice helped build teachers' confidence that the coach was there to support effective instructional practice. It also served to communicate that the principal was playing an active role and participating in the coaching partnership.

Even when the administrator has worked to build trust, there still may be teachers who are reluctant to participate in the coaching partnership. It is the administrator's role to encourage participation without undermining trust built by the coach and mentor. One way is to continually communicate the expectations for each member in the coaching partnership to improve school-wide student learning. Ongoing monitoring and reinforcement is often sufficient to build trust and increase participation in the partnership.

An effective instructional leader has a clear vision for improving teaching and learning. He or she works closely with the coach and mentor to achieve the vision. Frequent meetings with the coach and mentor will be the key to strengthening the administrator's role in facilitating collaborative coaching partnerships and achieving the vision. Meetings should take place with regularity and at a scheduled time. A protocol of topics should be identified so that the coaches and mentors arrive prepared and may include the following discussion:

- Teachers and groups that met in partnership with the coach over the past week;
- Key successes and progress toward learning goals;
- Key challenges, including scheduling, space, or needed resources that are inhibiting progress toward learning goals; and
- One to three action steps to be completed by the administrator and/or coach that will increase progress toward learning goals.

A collaborative relationship among coaches, mentors, and administrators will accelerate the impact of the partnership and will lead the school toward meeting student learning goals.

No doubt, time is the major obstacle to achieving successful learning outcomes for students and teachers. Administrators must be creative with time and scheduling. If adult learning is valued, then administrators will find ways to carve out time for opportunities for learners to observe each other, discuss learning, and analyze student evidence of learning. You may find ideas in the online resource from the Association of Supervision and Curriculum Development (ASCD), which offers creative ways to find time for professional learning: http://www.ascd.org/publications/educational-leadership/dec11/vol69/num04/Thinking-Outside-the-Box-and-Inside-the-Budget.aspx.

It is essential that the administrators model the behavior they desire to see in others. When the coach organizes professional learning sessions for large or small groups, the administrator should attend these whenever possible. Participation with teachers helps the administrator understand what he or she should be seeing and hearing in classrooms. First-hand observations of challenges associated with the coaching process and implementation of target instructional behaviors will assist the administrator in making decisions. By attending and participating in professional learning sessions, the administrator models the expectation that everyone participates in the coaching partnership.

Learning from experts on coaching, like Michael Fullan and Jim Knight, will help administrators cement their vision and role expectations within the coaching partnership. Videos from experts can be found at the Kansas University Center for Research on Learning: Instructional Coaching video archive (http://instructionalcoach.org/resources/video-archive) and are referenced at the end of this chapter.

SCENARIO: ROLES AND IMPLEMENTATION OF A READING INTERVENTION SOLUTION

It is September and the school district has adopted a new reading intervention for grades six, seven, and eight. The coaching goal is to improve reading teachers' effectiveness measured by students' reading achievement. To do so, expertise of school reading/literacy coaches and mentors and school district reading/literacy coaches will be developed to support the reading teachers' implementation.

The associate superintendent has contracted with a vendor to provide external coaching to the school and school district reading coaches and mentors who will, in turn, coach the reading teachers. Administrators were not included in the planning since the associate superintendent believes that they have enough to do without understanding what reading coaches and teachers will be doing.

The scenario begins with the vendor's external coaches providing group sessions for the school district and school coaches. The school district and school reading coaches will collaborate and coach side by side to assist one another in continuously improving and providing for consistency in language and messages to the reading teachers.

Felicia is the external coach and serves as the intervention expert and project manager. As such, she has taken a directive approach to her coaching and created a robust schedule of face-to-face professional learning sessions and classroom walkthroughs for school district coaches and school-based coaches. In addition, Felicia will provide monthly reports to the school district designee and meet with the associate superintendent four times a year to report on implementation and capacity-building progress.

Nicole is the lead school district coach. Nicole is doing her best to work with Felicia to coordinate the aggressive schedule of professional learning and coaching for the teachers and coaches. She is worried that the principals may not require their coaches to participate. In addition, she knows that the coaches are also responsible for supporting a new standards-based curriculum for all English language arts classrooms and is concerned about the time to support both initiatives simultaneously. She has directed the school district coaches that since the new curriculum will impact more teachers and students than the intervention, curriculum must be their first priority.

Cassandra has been selected as one of the reading intervention teachers. Although she has investigated the intervention program and found it to have a strong research base, she is not happy about the change in her assignment. She is an effective teacher and therefore her principal selected her to work with the students in reading intervention and asked for at least a one-year commitment to the program. She also heard that the external coach would be turning in reports to the school district designee and believes that her own effectiveness will not be brought to light. She is generally distrustful about this coaching partnership process.

Frank is the principal at Cassandra's school and knows that teachers are skeptical about the intervention, but the associate superintendent, Dr. George, asked him to make a special commitment to implementation and to possibly make his school a model one. Frank has aspirations of promotion to a school district-level position and wants to please Dr. George. On the other hand, he is worried about teacher buy-in and the ability of his school coach to support several simultaneous initiatives. Nevertheless, he directed the school coach, Albert, "Make it work!"

Albert, the school coach, is feeling overwhelmed. After school today, he is scheduled to be in two different places at the same time: report to the warehouse to pick up reading materials and go to the school district office to learn about the new curriculum. He wonders, "How will I be able to find time to coach the intervention teachers?"

Now, reflect on the scenario presented. While the topic is roles and implementation of a solution in reading intervention, the concepts may apply to any initiative's implementation—a new social studies textbook or a digital curriculum.

How would you suggest refining the roles for the reading teachers, school reading coaches and mentors, school district reading coaches, vendor's external coaches, and administrators?

Who will have more directive or less directive roles than the others?

How do you suggest arriving at consistency in academic language, understanding, and expertise among all in this complex partnership?

TIPS FOR PRODUCTIVE COACHING PARTNERSHIPS

Learner

Be confident in taking an active role in your own learning by assuredly communicating information that will assist in developing the coaching partnership. Expect a clear understanding of all aspects of the partnership: time, responsibilities, and expectations.

During the coaching process, keep an open mind and allow time for the process to work. Be metacognitive about the partnership experience and share reflections with the coach and mentor, including any doubts or concerns. By participating as an equal, active, willing, and committed partner, you as the learner will soon see your investment in personal professional learning pay off in the form of confidently delivered, highly effective, engaging instruction and improved student achievement.

Seek to understand the research supporting any expected implementation. Partner with external vendor coaches, school-based coaches, and mentors to explore the indicators of success and how those indicators might develop over time. Gain a clear mental model of expert implementation and take advantage of all available support.

Coach and Mentor

Do not be afraid to acknowledge when the identified coaching priority may be beyond your level of expertise. For example, if the priority requires you to have a deep understanding of how ELs acquire language, and that is currently not an area of expertise, ask for additional professional learning, or ask if the support can be assigned to another coach. Collaborate with your administrator to determine the coaching priority and format so that a plan can be created with that focus in mind. Continue to meet frequently with the administrator during the coaching process. Invite the administrator to experience classroom instruction for the priority areas side by side with you several times during the school year.

Once the coaching begins, clearly communicate your role and coaching purpose to the learner and administrator. Collaborate with the learner to develop the details of the partnership to achieve the stated priority. To learn more about how collaboration will build trust and deepen the coaching partnership relationship, read chapters 4 and 5.

Remember that coaches' and mentors' roles are often twofold: sometimes coaches and mentors take on the role of a learner to fully understand new expectations and are simultaneously in the role of coach and mentor facilitating others' implementation of new practices. Take advantage of school district coaches and external coaches when available. Maximize time with the other coaches to build your toolbox of resources and research-based practices to support teachers.

Finally, manage time well. Ask your administrator to protect your time so that it is not used for noncoaching tasks. Coaches and mentors with different roles are to clarify the differences and communicate to all in the partnership. Think about making a t-chart or venn diagram to graphically depict how the roles overlap and how they are different.

Administrator

Establish a rationale, common understanding, and vision for the coaching partnership and communicate it consistently. To this end, do not underestimate the value of time invested in collaboration with the coach and mentor to determine the coaching priority before the coaching process begins. By investing time upfront, the roles for the coach and mentor, learner, and administrator can be defined, allowing you to clearly communicate expectations to all stakeholders.

During the coaching process, continue to provide time for professional learning: study groups, peer observations, coaching debriefs, co-planning, co-teaching, lesson modeling, and analysis of evidence of learning. In addition, develop the habit of monitoring and encouraging participation in the coaching partnership through consistent and positive communication that reinforces and celebrates observed research-based practices.

With new implementations, take on the role of both learner and leader. Know the instructional components and practices to look for during classroom walkthroughs and provide explicit feedback. Build a culture that embraces change and sets expectations for success.

Even as the coaching partnership continues, invest time by modeling the importance of professional learning through attendance and active participation. Schedule regular meetings with the coach and mentor to monitor progress and offer support. Take advantage of faculty meetings, e-mail, newsletters, intranets, etc., to encourage participation in the coaching partnership. By committing time to the partnership, the trust and vision necessary to create a culture of professional learning as the path to improved student learning will be established.

REFLECTIVE PRACTICE FOR ESTABLISHING ROLES

Reflection is a recommended professional practice for all in the partnership. This chapter has focused on developing the coach and mentor, learner, and administrator roles for successful coaching partnerships. These reflection activities guide partners through the process for clearly defining and communicating roles to establish common understandings and expectations for all. Coaches, mentors, and administrators are encouraged to complete Tables 2.1 and 2.2 together and agree upon priorities and roles for the coaching partnership. Most likely, these areas are informed by evidence and data on student learning and teacher effectiveness. Also, turn to Appendix A and reflect on how actions define your role.

Table 2.1   Reflection and Commitment to Action

Questions	Priority
What are school or school district priorities?	
What are the school district or school initiatives?	
What is the standards-based curriculum priority?	
What student population is the greatest priority? (e.g., English Learners, Special Education Students, General Education Students, Grade Level)	
How will success be measured? (e.g., accountability assessment, progress monitoring, formative assessment, surveys, student evidence)	
How much of the coach's or mentor's time will be dedicated to working on the priority commitments to action?	

Source: Rosemarye T. Taylor & Carol Chanter.

Table 2.2   Role Agreement: Coach, Mentor, Learner, and Administrator

Role	Agreements
Coaching and Mentoring Priority	
Professional Assets	
Time frame and Time Commitment	
Learner's Goals	
Role of Reflection	
Documentation and Communication Protocol	
Intended Outcomes/Benefits	
Directive or Reflective	

Source: Rosemarye T. Taylor & Carol Chanter.

DEFINITIONS

School Coach   Teacher leader who has the responsibility to promote improvement in teacher effectiveness and student learning for one school.

School District Coach	Teacher leader who has the responsibility to promote improvement in teacher effectiveness and student learning for one district.
External Coach	Consultant who has the responsibility to promote improvement in teacher effectiveness and student learning.
Capacity Building	Planned development of knowledge and skills to support self-development and that of others.
Fidelity	Implementation aligned with the research upon which the model or strategy was designed and tested.
Novice Teacher	A teacher new to the field or new to a particular grade level or content area.
Metacognitive	Being aware of one's own thought processes.

RESOURCES

Aguilar, E. (2015, May 17). The Art of Coaching Teachers. [Web log]. Retrieved from http://blogs.edweek.org/teachers/coaching_teachers/.

Kansas University Center for Research on Learning. Instructional Coaching: Kansas Coaching Project. [Video Archive]. (2015, May 17). Retrieved from http://instructionalcoach.org/resources/video-archive.

Killion, J. & Harrison, C. (2006). *Taking the Lead: New Roles for Teachers and School-Based Coaches.* Oxford, OH: National Staff Development Council.

Literacy Coaching Clearinghouse. Teacher Survey/Coaching Request Form (2015, May 17). Retrieved from http://www.literacycoachingonline.org.

Literacy Coaching Clearinghouse. Coaching Self-Assessment for Elementary Literacy Coaches. (2015, May 17). Retrieved from http://www.literacycoachingonline.org.

Literacy Coaching Clearinghouse. Coaching Self Assessment for Middle and High School Literacy Coaches. (2015, May 17). Retrieved from http://www.literacycoachingonline.org.

Sweeney, D. (February 2010–March 2015). Student Centered Coaching blog. 69(4). [Web Log]. Retrieved from http://dianesweeney.com/student-centered-coaching-blog/.

Yendol-Hoppey, D. & Fichtman-Dana, N. (December 2011/January 2012). The resourceful school: Thinking outside the box and inside the budget. Retrieved from http://www.ascd.org/publications/educational-leadership/dec11/vol69/num04/Thinking-Outside-the-Box-and-Inside-the-Budget.aspx.

Chapter 3

Generative Thinking

To bring about reasoning, imagining, reflection, and intention is to open the world of the possible. When you are open to new possibilities, new ways of thinking, and new ways of doing, you open the door to higher achievement for students. This is a description of *generative thinking*.

Generative thinking is a disposition that is the premise underpinning the relationship building, communication, coaching process, and continual development of expertise. The term "generative" means to develop and continue in an iterative manner. Generative thinking encourages learning and inquiry. It is grounded in the belief that everyone can develop thinking and hence professional expertise (Puig & Froelich, 2011).

The generative dispositions brought to the partnership demonstrate belief in the potential of others. Generative thinking is reflected in open-ended inquiry-based professional practice that supports the generation of thinking (Puig & Froelich, 2011). Yes or no questions or directive responses are non-examples of generative thinking. The authors' assumption is that by probing carefully with generative inquiry, metacognition will be enhanced to continually develop expertise of adult learners and students.

UNCOVERING PERSONAL THINKING DISPOSITIONS

Coaches, mentors, learners, and administrators may be unaware of the dispositions they bring to the coaching partnership. Improvement in effectiveness will be accelerated when belief in the development potential of each through research-based support and hard work is central to partnership thinking.

The first step in being able to generate thinking is to uncover your own dispositions about thinking and learning. Uncovering dispositions means to determine beliefs about your own learning, the learning of students, and the learning of other adults. If you believe that ability and intelligence are not fixed, there is much to learn, and ways in which to grow, then you have an open thinking disposition. You, the coach, mentor, learner, or administrator are ready to learn from peers, professional learning, and from students.

Generative thinking enables coaches, mentors, learners, and administrators to embrace learning and behavioral challenges with adults and students as opportunities for success. When thinking is open, practitioners ask, "What can I do to make a difference in this student's or educator's learning? Is there something that I can change in my instruction or communication that will facilitate this individual's success?" Recognition that learners are expected to ask questions and that important problems may be without immediate solutions stimulates inquiry.

In her blog post, Education 3.0: Altering Round Peg in Round Hole Education (2013), Jackie Gerstein provides examples of open and closed thinking dispositions. Table 3.1 is based on Gerstein (2013) and is a reflection tool for you to review and to consider in developing open-ended thinking communication. There are a number of resources that may be useful in uncovering thinking patterns, including several self-assessment tools, which can be found at (http://www.mindsetworks.com/assess/and http://mindsetonline.com/testyourmindset/step1.php).

Table 3.1   Examples of Closed and Open Thinking Dispositions

Closed Thinking Dispositions	Open Thinking Dispositions
I don't have enough time.	I can use technology to make both my own and my students' learning richer.
I don't have enough resources.	I can make one small change at a time in my learning environment.
I need more preparation and support.	I can network and connect with others for resources, assistance, and support.
I need to teach using the textbook.	I can risk trying new learning tasks.
I need to teach to the test.	I can bring my passion and my students' passions into learning tasks.
I might lose control of the class.	I can let go of my need to control all classroom variables.
I have always been successful in teaching this way.	I value my relationships with my students.

Source: Rosemarye T. Taylor & Carol Chanter (Gerstein, 2013).

FOSTERING GENERATIVE THINKING IN OTHERS

How can coaches, mentors, learners, and administrators foster generative thinking? Thinking dispositions are learned through a process of enculturation, rather than through direct instruction (Tishman, et al., 1995; Tishman & Perkins, 1997). Professional behaviors develop in response to extended exposure to a particular culture of learning and result in one's thinking dispositions. If the cultural norm is for responses or actions to be judged as either right or wrong, then closed thinking may be the disposition.

A closed thinking disposition can be rooted in experiences outside of school or in early learning experiences. It is up to coaches, mentors, learners, and administrators to reveal the potential of every learner. By doing so, you create a culture that fosters development of generative thinking.

To develop a culture of inquiry and continuous improvement, create structures that provide time and opportunity. Encourage others to try out new learning, make mistakes risk free, and participate in self-reflection. Develop a safe environment to support generative thinking. Learning structures such as lesson study, learning walks, peer collaboration, and coaching can be opportunities for learners to practice new professional behaviors. In safe professional learning experiences, learners can meet challenges with support and without judgment.

Modeling of expectations is an effective means of encouraging adults and students to view themselves as capable learners. By modeling desirable dispositions and beliefs in learners' abilities, you assist others in adopting the same beliefs and dispositions. Group practice with challenges or problems of practice scenarios can generate thinking of potential solutions and professional behaviors. Sharing examples of changed thinking and asking open-ended questions also model generative thinking. Inquiry examples will be similar to, "What would happen if . . .?" A nonexample of generative thinking would be, "It would be better to . . . ."

Finally, by emphasizing the developmental nature of learning, highlighting the role and reward of hard work, and inviting participation of the learner, generative thinking will be the central idea of learning. When generative thinking is a foundational belief, it is meaningful and observable in professional practice.

Developing a culture of generative thinking takes time and effort by coaches, mentors, learners, and administrators. However, the benefits for learners can extend far beyond the individual classroom, school, or professional experience.

GENERATIVE THINKING FRAMEWORK

Even within a well-established culture of generative thinking, learners may still need support and scaffolding to facilitate continual improvement of expertise.

The authors propose a framework to encourage generative thinking which supports each chapter that follows. The acronym EASY (evidence, analysis, solutions to explore, and yes agreements) may help to frame open-ended comments to scaffold and support generative thinking.

Evidence

Think about how to generate thoughts related to evidence of student learning. What types of student language, behavior, work, or data can be identified that will help to guide the coaching conversation? Three or more evidences should always be considered.

Analyze

Analyze the evidences to identify commonalities, trends, or differences. Consider other data or evidence needed as a basis of inquiry or a problem of practice to potentially solve.

Solutions to Explore

Identify research-based potential solutions or strategies that respond to the inquiry or problem of practice identified.

Yes Agreement

Think about how to determine and agree upon next steps that may lead to the most efficacious solution.

After reviewing the generative thinking within EASY, consider the examples in Table 3.2 that a coach, mentor, or administrator may employ with a learner.

Table 3.2   EASY Examples to Foster Generative Thinking

Evidence	Analysis	Solutions to Explore	Yes Agreements to Next Steps
What was most effective? How do you know?	Which evidences of effectiveness will you review?	The potential solutions are. . .	Of the potential solutions, which will you try?
The evidences made me wonder _____.	What did you do that worked well?	What will you do the same or differently?	What is possible to try before we meet again?
How do you know who met and did not meet the goal?	What do evidence and data tell us?	How will you expand upon your success?	What do you need to achieve the intended outcome?
What did you notice about _____?	Based on the evidence, who met the learning goal?	What do you need to do for . . . to achieve mastery?	What could be your first step?

As you review the examples, frame EASY as a process that naturally moves from (1) Evidence to (2) Analysis to (3) Solutions to Explore to (4) Yes Agreements.

SCENARIO: EMBRACING A GENERATIVE THINKING CULTURE

Coaching and mentoring partnerships are most successful when all partners embrace the belief that learning and achievement depend on more than assets brought to the setting. Results will be greatest when each believes that his or her individual abilities can be further developed through reflection, research-based support, and hard work. Read through the scenario and think about how school culture and coaching partnerships can impact generative thinking.

Jennifer, a seventh-grade mathematics teacher, recently interviewed for a position with Principal Rodriguez and was invited to transfer to Central Middle School. In her previous school, teachers rarely collaborated and the principal expected everyone to just do their jobs. Professional learning opportunities were rare and were in the format of daylong sessions with national experts speaking about their preferred processes and those they had found to work. This format was primarily due to the financial investment that these national experts represented and the need for experts to interact with as many as possible while at that school. The purpose was broad dissemination of the knowledge of the experts.

Conversations in the teachers' lounge had centered on the demographic changes in the community and on low expectations for students' performance on the state assessments. Jennifer hoped that the student behavior and achievement would be better at Central Middle School. She was very disappointed to learn that she would be teaching seventh-grade mathematics instead of the Algebra I classes that she had been promised during the interview.

After the first month of school, Jennifer was more convinced than ever that her mathematics students were not capable of mastering the new state standards and the standards of mathematical practice. She began to dread the year ahead, and she longed for the day she could teach Algebra I or even Geometry. She believed that her students were doing their best and not capable of learning more.

After the first six-week benchmark assessment results were in, the mathematics coach, Bernard, approached Jennifer and shared that he would value the opportunity to support her. Bernard offered to model an algebraic reasoning lesson that was aligned with the upcoming target mathematics standard. Jennifer was hesitant but reluctantly agreed. After all, she could use the break from trying to engage uninterested students. Before modeling the lesson,

Bernard asked Jennifer to complete a self-reflection so that he could learn more about her students and her teaching strategies.

Feeling regretful that she had agreed to the coach modeling with her students, she went to the teachers' lounge and joined her team teachers. She inquired about Bernard to learn if any of the other teachers had experienced his coaching. Jennifer was surprised by the overwhelmingly positive response from her colleagues. Several expressed how helpful Bernard had been. Linda, who had also taught the same seventh-grade mathematics course last year, recounted how when she had first come to the school, Bernard had modeled a lesson and afterward they had been engaged in a great discussion. She advocated for coaching: "Bernard has a knack for asking just the right questions that really make you think about your teaching and how the students respond. I used to think that they just couldn't grasp the more complex mathematical concepts, but in the past two years in the coaching partnership with Bernard, my students' proficiency scores have increased by 30 percent. These kids really can learn mathematics and enjoy being successful with mathematics!"

Linda then invited Jennifer to observe her instruction and shared that the principal encouraged colleagues to observe one another. In fact, the principal would provide coverage for Jennifer's class while she visited Linda's class.

The discussion with Linda stimulated Jennifer to reflect. Never had anyone at her previous school invited her to observe. Nor had anyone offered to model instruction with her students. She began to realize that Central Middle School was different from her former school. She wondered, "Is it possible that my students can master the challenging standards?"

Jennifer completed the self-reflection requested by Bernard. She surprised herself when she realized that by responding to the open-ended and generative statements, she gained new insight into her instruction. The day before Bernard was scheduled to model the lesson, he met with Jennifer and asked which mathematical instructional strategies she would like to see modeled and if there were any particular students that she would like him to target for engagement. In addition, he reviewed with her a lesson observation feedback tool and invited her to complete it while he modeled. Jennifer had not watched anyone teach since she completed her teacher preparation program and certainly had never provided feedback. She wondered, "How will this experience turn out?"

The day came for Bernard to model the lesson. Jennifer had prewarned the students that there would be a guest teacher and cautioned them to behave well. The lesson began, and Jennifer was amazed by the amount of time Bernard devoted to student collaboration. She rarely allowed the students to talk or work in groups because she was concerned that they would not focus on the learning task. Much to her surprise, the students not only behaved well, they also seemed more intellectually engaged than during her teaching. She knew they were engaged by evidence that included asking clarifying questions. They were working intensely to solve more challenging word problems than she had included in her instructional plans.

After the modeled lesson, Bernard arranged for a classroom assistant to monitor the students so that he and Jennifer could reflect together and collaborate. Bernard asked Jennifer, "What did you notice related to the student work and student interactions?" He allowed her time to reflect on what she had noticed and how his teaching strategies resulted in more students being intellectually engaged. Bernard asked her if she would like to continue the coaching partnership. With Jennifer's affirmative response, they agreed to co-plan the next standards-based lesson and co-teach it as well. Jennifer was amazed at how energized she felt by the experience and how much she was looking forward to co-planning and co-teaching. She wondered, "Could I have misjudged these students?"

Reflect on Jennifer's scenario. In what ways did her colleagues, Principal Rodriguez and Coach Bernard, display generative thinking dispositions? Reread and highlight the language that was used to model generative thinking, along with standards-based and evidence-based instruction.

In contrast, have you experienced a closed, nongenerative thinking culture? In a school culture where generative thinking is not the norm, suggest steps for administrators, coaches, mentors, and teachers to take for initiating change to a generative thinking culture. Jot down your first two steps.

TIPS FOR A GENERATIVE THINKING COACHING PARTNERSHIP

Learner

Learners come to embrace the belief that the ability to learn and achieve is not static and can be developed through effort. They share their belief with their students and model the belief through their professional language and behaviors. Becoming metacognitive about the formative learning process will open the door to positive change for both the adult learner and the students. During the coaching partnership, learners strive to remember that thoughts and reactions are valid, including doubts and fears. Staying in touch with feelings and thoughts during the coaching process and trusting the coach or mentor enough to share them will help generate thinking that is productive and that results in action.

Use the power of modeling generative thinking and belief in the development of intelligence with students. Assure that each student has the same opportunities for success through differentiated support and recognition of growth. Investigate some of the free resources for students found at https://www.mindsetworks.com/free-resources/log-in-or-free-signup.aspx.

Remember that reflecting, responding, and asking questions that generate thinking will scaffold you, as a learner, to be an active and equal partner in the coaching and mentoring process. Learners who are generative thinkers often leave the coaching session thinking, "I am ready to try something new," or "I can't wait to find out how my students will respond to this approach," or "I wondered if my teaching was effective and now I know, because the coaching validated me as a professional. I am more confident."

Coach and Mentor

Great coaches and mentors are experts in leading with inquiry, that is, in asking generative questions or making generative statements that lead to new thinking and self-efficacy. Remember that a generative thinking disposition is the premise underpinning the entirety of the coaching and mentoring partnership. Coaches and mentors are to facilitate structures for inquiry in which generative thinking is used to encourage learning and inquiry. Coaches and mentors model beliefs that everyone can develop thinking and hence their expertise. Act with the belief that intelligence and achievement can be developed, including your own.

Administrators

Administrators are responsible for creating and sustaining a culture that facilitates generative thinking. Risk-taking and even mistake-making are viewed as a natural part of growing professionally. It is as important to know what does not work well as what does work well.

To create a generative thinking culture, consistently model the belief that intelligence and achievement can be developed and that effort yields results. Offer examples from your own professional experiences and the experiences of teachers and students who have embraced generative thinking. By sharing examples of those who exceeded the expectations they had for themselves, as well as those expectations held by others, you are providing models for others to emulate. Challenge other administrators, faculty, and staff by modeling what-if thinking and questions leading to a commitment to action. Ask questions like "What if . . . ?" "Which of your actions resulted in students exceeding your expectations?" and, "What action will you take today that will make a positive difference in at least one student's achievement?"

REFLECTIVE PRACTICE FOR GENERATIVE THINKING

You have read chapters 1 through 3 and are now grounded in the foundation for successful coaching partnerships. In chapter 1, you conceptualized a practical systematic approach for coaches, mentors, learners, and administrators to influence each other's effectiveness. Greater student achievement will result by holding each other mutually accountable for student learning and for each other's growth.

In chapter 2, you considered the complex roles of coaches, mentors, learners, and administrators that impact decisions about the coaching partnership. Also, you reflected on the importance of attending to roles to set up the partnership for the greatest success. In this chapter, you explored generative thinking as a disposition underpinning relationship building, communication, coaching process, and continual development of expertise that follow in the next chapters.

Consider your learning by completing the reflection frame independently or collaboratively with your partnership team.

In my role as a_____ one thing I will do to develop and support a culture of generative thinking is_____.

I will support the development of generative thinking in others and in myself in these ways.

1. _____
2. _____
3. _____

DEFINITIONS

Generative Thinking	The process of generating new ideas through inquiry and open-ended statements. It reflects a belief in the continual development of ability of self and others.
Ability	Talent, skill, or proficiency in a particular area.
Achievement	Success resulting from effort and self-belief, courage, or skill.
Disposition	Attitude or belief brought to the learning context; the natural or developed mental and emotional outlook or expectation for learning.

RESOURCES

Mindset Assessments. (August 9, 2015). Retrieved from http://www.mindsetworks. com/assess/.

Mindset. (August 9, 2015). Retrieved from http://mindsetonline.com/testyourmind-set/step1.php.

Mindset Works. (August 9, 2015). Retrieved from https://www.mindsetworks.com/ free-resources/log-in-or-free-signup.aspx.

Puig, E. A. & Froelich, K. S. (2011). *The Literacy Coach: Guiding in the Right Direc-tion* (2nd edition). Boston: Pearson/Allyn & Bacon.

Chapter 4

Relationships

Building relationships as a chapter topic has been developed at the request of coaches and administrators, who told the authors that "everyone tells us that we need to build relationships, but how do you do it? How do you build trust?" As you read, you may think that relationship building is a natural process necessary to coaching and to leadership. Even so, the authors' intent is that you reflect and validate the relationship-building behaviors that you employ and think about those that you may want to build upon.

Relationships are central to any partnership. Think about how you and your best friends or colleagues interact and the rapport that you enjoy.

- Are you guarded or open in what you share?
- Do you believe that they are confident of your positive intent?
- Are you honest with one another or do you refrain from authentic communication?
- What has to take place before you allow yourself to take risks and even be vulnerable?

TRUST

In most cases, the main criterion that is needed for you to be open and authentic in communication and to be confident of positive intent and allows you to accept feedback is trust. When you understand people well enough that you trust them, then there is less risk to share openly, to ask for assistance, or to admit that you have areas for improvement. The need is to know how to build trust. Trust is built through predictability, modeling, communication, and competence.

Predictability

Trust has been referred to as the glue that holds any organization together. Schools and school districts are no exceptions. Trust is built through consistent and predictable actions.

A few years ago, there was a school district leader who was well respected and would tell principals not to worry, "I have your back!" Then, he would return to the school district office and say demeaning things about a principal who had confided in him. Colleagues knew that they could not trust this person, although he was predictable. They learned not to share or be vulnerable in their conversations with him or in his presence as mutual trust was limited by his predictable behaviors.

On the other hand, the colleague who you can trust and who does not share your confidences with others is also predictable. Think of the person you go to for feedback or to gain dependable perspectives. Is this person predictable in how he or she will respond to confidences? Are these shared with others? Trust is built upon predictability in ways that advance the relationship.

An area of predictability to consider is taking action when concerns are raised. The coaching partnership is dependent upon action steps or professional behaviors. When the learner, administrator, coach, or mentor has received a concern, predictably taking actions goes far in building trust. The one who receives a concern and takes no action is also predictable, but this person will not have a high trust level with others.

In the coaching partnership, each will learn about strengths and weaknesses of the others in the partnership. The commitment to each other's improvement also has to have commitment of positive intent and predictable discretion in the use of what is learned. The roles developed in chapter 2 should include the expectation of confidentiality and with whom information will be shared.

Modeling

Leaders have an important role in setting expectations and modeling their value of expectations through their actions. If the coach, mentor, or administrator shares that he has a coach to support his instructional leadership skill development, then it stands to reason that others in the school may also have a coach to develop their skills. As a leader, you know that others take cues on what is acceptable and what is not from you. If you consistently arrive at work early and stay late, others will also. On the other hand, if you put down the students or their families, others who observe the behavior, will believe it is acceptable, and may adopt the same behaviors, handicapping the development of a generative disposition, as shared in chapter 3.

For the administrator, coach, or mentor, modeling of professional expectations is essential. Are you always where you say you will be? Do you arrive at scheduled coaching and mentoring sessions on time and give 100 percent attention to the learner? Do you reschedule mentoring and coaching sessions frequently? The professional expectations of the learner are to be modeled by the coach and mentor, as well as by the administrator.

Learners also develop trust with the administrator, coach, and mentor. Do you arrive on time to coaching and mentoring sessions with the data or evidences that are needed? After the mentoring sessions, do you follow-through with the agreed-upon action steps? Demonstrating trust with others (from learner's perspective) that you are working to improve expertise in the essential components builds the relationship in the partnership.

Communication

Trust is built by treating others respectfully and listening to them with respect. In chapter 5, listening to others with an open mind and considering their perspectives are noted as important. Besides being an example of effective adult communication, listening and empathizing also builds trust. These professional behaviors let the speaker know that you value them, what they think, and what they say.

Competence

To be able to trust in someone's communication, modeling, coaching, or feedback, people have to believe that the individual in question is competent. Within the coaching partnership, the competence needed is in the five essential areas of expertise noted in chapter 1 and in leadership for the administrators. Trusting in what a person says to be true or in how he or she coaches, mentors, and leads is dependent upon believing that that person is competent and has research-based expertise. Expert power and influence does not depend upon title or position but on knowledge, skill, and credibility.

RAPPORT

Even if you trust one another, it will be difficult to have a productive professional relationship if you do not get along or have rapport with one another. Specific action steps can be taken to build rapport for forging purposeful relationships. Include purposeful pre-meetings before coaching and mentoring begin to clarify roles and the focus of the partnership. Getting to know the person in each role through inquiry is also a good strategy. What would you want to know if you were invited to be a coach, mentor, learner, or administrator in a coaching partnership? Sample inquiry statements might be similar to those bulleted.

- I wonder, how or why you became a coach?
- What can you tell me about your motivation to be an instructional science coach, instead of a physical science teacher?
- Your reputation precedes you as having high expectations. I am wondering if I can meet those high expectations.
- What can I do to support your effectiveness (administrator, coach, mentor, or teacher)?
- What would you like to know about me as an educator/leader/coach?
- You seem a little anxious. What can I do to alleviate your concern?

For in-person meetings, always prepare an agenda or a list of inquiries that you have. This way you will not forget what you wanted to tell and what you wanted to ask. It also provides you a safe place to note responses and you have your notes for future reference in case you have a forgetful moment.

In-person meetings are the best way to discuss controversial or sensitive concerns. Certainly, never put confidential or personal information in an e-mail or other digital communication. To overcome barriers or any negative experience, in-person is recommended over e-mail, if only for the ease with which e-mail can be misunderstood.

Celebrations are also best held in-person. With this said, quick e-mail or electronic follow-ups and confirmations of success can serve as reminders of the growth and positive results that the partnership has yielded. Personal complimentary communications and handwritten notes also go a long way to communicate that the person is worth the time. Mass e-mails, form letters, or notes written by a designee do not serve the same purpose and suggest that the recipient is not valued enough to give of one's own time and energy.

Digital tools and social media can be used to build on in-person meetings. With the many tools available, quick digital communications can save time so that in-person time is strategically leveraged for important items and for discussions that are better in person than in e-mail or via other digital records. However, be cautious of depending upon quick e-mail communication as you can easily reduce the relationship to an impersonal one with notes read without benefit of your smile, positive tone, and clarification.

Above all, in communications, demonstrate fairness and respect. For the coaching partnership to thrive, there can be no lack of respect. Fairness has to be present. Recently, after a classroom walkthrough, a social studies teacher exclaimed to his principal, "You are *not* a blank slate!" Initially, the administrator chuckled a little in embarrassment but then realized that the social studies teacher was surprised that as an administrator he knew social studies inquiry strategies. The teacher was inferring that administrators were judged as not having relevant knowledge. Although no malice was intended, the teacher was not being respectful nor fair to others with the backhanded comment. Each person in the partnership is to be treated respectfully and fairly without judgment.

COACHING PARTNERSHIP RELATIONSHIP

Developing the coach and mentor-learner relationship, teacher-administrator relationship, and coach-administrator relationship are all equally important. Adopting equality and reciprocity as founding principles for the coaching relationship will aid in building trust to accelerate the coaching process. Keep in mind that there are times when there may be a hierarchical relationship between the administrator and the coach or teacher. In the coaching partnership, all are equal in asking for, receiving, and giving coaching and feedback. Reciprocity and equality should be accompanied by reciprocal accountability or accountability that is mutually owned for one another's effectiveness and continual growth.

Scenario: Establishing Rapport

Instructional coach Vernita has an appointment with Principal Glenn to build rapport, establish mutual expectations for her time use, and to determine focus for coaching. She had learned at instructional coaching professional learning that this was the first step to take to be an effective coach. Vernita arrives at the appointed time and learns that Principal Glenn is not on the school campus, so she waits in his office.

After about 20 minutes, Glenn arrives and apologizes for not being punctual. Immediately, he tells Vernita that she is the coach and he wants her to do what she thinks is best. Then, he follows with, "The mathematics scores have to increase this year! If not, we may lose more high performing students and families from our school." Vernita thinks for a moment and then seeks clarification, "Are you saying that the focus for coaching this year should be on improvement of reading and mathematics achievement?" The principal responded that his priority for the year was mathematics and indicated that he had another appointment in 10 minutes and asked, "What else do we need to discuss so that you can begin coaching?"

Vernita was a little confused, because she had hoped to have time to review disaggregated achievement data by student groups and by teachers. She had in mind the purpose of identifying the teachers for priority coaching, the students who needed the most improvement, and the standards on which to focus. She wanted to have a substantive conversation with Principal Glenn about his expectations for her and his understanding of the coaching process, but she could see that he wanted to proceed to his next appointment.

Developing a positive rapport with Glenn was essential, so she chose to close the discussion on a positive note, "I appreciate the direction you have given me. We know that students who do not do well on the mathematics assessment also do not read at proficiency and miss the word problems. What would you think about combining reading and mathematics as a focus to improve mathematics scores? I am happy to draft a plan, based on the available data and meet with you again soon to get your feedback." Glenn was relieved that Vernita seemed to know exactly what to do: "Great idea! Yes, how about in a few days let's talk again and maybe invite a few highly effective teachers, who are also mentors, to join us and get their feedback?" Vernita did not achieve her goals for the meeting, but she and Glenn learned a little about each other. Because she was well prepared for the meeting, she was able to be flexible and adjust quickly and smoothly as Glenn steered the conversation toward a shorter than anticipated meeting.

- What was accomplished during the conversation?
- What did each learn about the coaching partnership, about the other, and about working together?
- What would you say to Vernita if you were her coach?
- What would you say to Principal Glenn if you were his principal coach?
- Hypothesize how the rapport may develop.

TIPS FOR POSITIVE RELATIONSHIPS IN THE COACHING PARTNERSHIP

Sometimes it can be challenging when you are in a reciprocally accountable relationship, such as the coaching partnership. It is easy to fall into a pattern of casual and social conversation or in being overly blunt, which may reduce the trust among the partners. To facilitate authentic discussions that build rapport and trust, while delving into the evidence you noticed, gathered, and analyzed, think about how to use inquiry.

The authors suggest deleting the common, "Any questions?" and replacing the query with, "Jot down your wonders." The rationale for this suggestion is that having a question may signal a lack of knowledge or expertise. On the other hand, highly accomplished people think and wonder. Those who make a great impact on the world, like Bill Gates, wonder. After classroom walkthroughs or analysis of evidence and data, have a partnership discussion and offer *wonderings*, *noticings*, and *what-ifs*. During partnership discussions, use stems that have no inference of judgment, such as the following.

- I am wondering . . .
- I am curious about . . .
- Did you notice . . . ?
- Please share your noticings.
- I noticed . . .
- What would happen if . . . ?

Learner

Develop a critical friend relationship with the coach and mentor, who may or may not be in your work site. Critical friends are often in other work sites or have different positions (e.g., coach, mentor, administrator) and therefore have views different from yours. Critical friends are those who are willing to provide authentic feedback and ask questions that others may not be willing to raise. In other words, critical friends are your advocates who care enough about your success to challenge and deepen your thinking, analysis, and evaluation (Costa & Kallick, 1993).

Expect the relationship to develop instructional pedagogical skills and make a positive difference in student learning outcomes. Trust the coaching process. Reciprocally, model professional behaviors that build rapport and trust with the members of the partnership.

Coach and Mentor

Deliberately build positive relationships with both the learner and the administrator. Take action to build trust and rapport through professional modeling of expectations, expertise, and predictability. Make commitments that you can keep. Follow-up on every coaching or mentoring session and request. Be prepared to adjust your agenda to align with the agenda of the administrator.

Administrator

Value and develop the relationship with the coach and mentor. The coach and mentor can provide a lens through which you can view the culture of the school and school district. They can reveal deeply held beliefs aligned with behaviors or decisions that are barriers to improvement. Once you recognize barriers, collaborate to determine action steps to remove the barriers.

Administrators often have dual roles of evaluator while being a member in the coaching partnership. The duality of roles can create conflict. For a productive coaching partnership, focus on your role as an equal member of the coaching partnership, since that will improve student learning. Evaluation has not shown the same promise as coaching.

Be clear when you are evaluating and when you are coaching for continuous improvement. Because you may also have the role of evaluator, be mindful of how communications may be received or the tone that may be inferred, even if not intended. Carefully and purposefully select the mode of communication. Whenever possible, take time to handwrite notes of appreciation and acknowledgment of forward improvement.

REFLECTIVE PRACTICE IN RELATIONSHIP BUILDING

Learners, coaches, mentors, and administrators each may want to be metacognitive about how to deliberately and purposefully develop rapport, trust, and credibility. Listen, ask thoughtful questions, view through various lenses, and reframe situations to arrive at the best possible strategies for creating positive relationships. Turn to Appendix A and review the row, Relationships, chapter 4. Reflect regularly on your relationships with those in the coaching partnership.

- How do you go about developing rapport?
- Do you give others your undivided attention?
- How do you demonstrate respect for each person in the partnership?
- Think of examples when you did not show your negative or disapproving thinking on your face or with your body language. What did you say or do to turn the negative response into a generative response to build the relationship?
- How often do you think about noticing instead of evaluating when you visit classrooms or interact with those in the coaching partnership?

DEFINITIONS

Critical friend	Professional advocate who provides authentic perspectives.
Equality	Expectation for thinking and sharing is the same for each.
Rapport	Comfortable relationship.
Reciprocity	Accepted mutual accountability for outcomes (See reciprocal accountability, chapter 7).
Trust	Confidence in the predictability of another's behavior.

RESOURCES

Fink, S. & Markholt, A. (2011). *Leading for Instructional Improvement: How Successful Leaders Develop Teaching and Learning Expertise.* San Francisco: Jossey-Bass.

Harris, S. & Edmondson, S. (2013). *The Trust Factor: Strategies for School Leaders.* New York: Routledge.

Robertson, J. (2008). *The 3 Rs for Coaching Learning Relationships: Policy and Practice.* PDF. http://www.educationalleaders.govt.nz/Leadership-development/Professional-information/Considering-principalship/Mentoring-and-coaching/Coaching-Learning-Relationships.

Chapter 5

Effective Adult Communication

Even with productive relationships, clear roles, deep content knowledge, and expertise in pedagogy, the coaching partnership's success to change student learning may rely on expertise with adult communication strategies (Mangin & Dunsmore, 2015). As in the other chapters in this text, coach refers to mentor and coach and effectiveness refers to improvement of student learning.

Coaches and mentors generally support individual teachers unless their role is defined as school improvement and they are supporting large groups of teachers. There are a number of models of effective adult communication. One of the most widely accepted models of one-to-one adult coaching communication is that of Costa and Garmston (1994), and it is called cognitive coaching.

In contrast, those who impact school-wide change in student learning frequently communicate with groups of adults in collaborative planning, curriculum alignment, or other strategic processes. All improve the instructional process and student learning outcomes school-wide or school district-wide. With appropriate adjustments, the same kinds of adult communication strategies can be effectively implemented with individuals and groups.

This chapter begins with the concepts of effective adult communication strategies and academic language followed by a scenario in the practice of education. Next are tips for learners, coaches and mentors, and administrators, followed by communicative reflective practice. Definitions of academic language in this chapter and resources that may support communication for productive coaching partnerships complete the chapter.

EFFECTIVE ADULT COMMUNICATION STRATEGIES

Communication is influenced by how the coaching and mentoring role is framed. If it is framed as directive, then giving specific expectations would be the appropriate strategy. In this text, the goal of coaching and mentoring is reflective practice and metacognition of the learner so that continual improvement occurs, even when the coach or mentor is not present. Adult communication is focused on developing the adult learners' reflective thinking (Mangin & Dunsmore, 2015).

First and foremost, coaches, mentors, learners, and administrators have to develop a common language with common understanding of the terms that will be used in their specific context. As an example, at the end of each chapter, academic language is defined as used in this text.

In a school setting, effective coaching communication may be defined as facilitating the learner's reflection leading to next steps. A nonexample of effective coaching communication would be directing or telling learners what they must do. Exceptions would be in the case of safety or potential harm to students. Supporting this concept of effective adult communication is the notion of role differentiation, as noted in chapter 2. Supervision, which at times includes directing, generally is the responsibility of administrators and not that of coaches or mentors.

Effective adult communication strategies include norms of collaboration, mind and body alignment, active listening, empathizing, generative response, and co-construction of strength-based action steps using academic language. Coaches, mentors, and administrators do not have to have answers. Their role is to help others find potential solutions. In doing so, they model that they also are continually learning. Effective coach and mentor-learner communications are progressively more focused, with deeper thinking, and more reflection leading to action steps.

Norms of Collaboration

All cultures have norms, and in schools norms are evidenced by professional practices and habits of those in the school. Most probably norms were not purposefully decided upon but just developed over time. As an example, in some schools adults refer to each other by their last names (Taylor) rather than by first names (Rose). In other schools, many teachers either work beyond the stipulated hour or all leave precisely at the allotted time. Such things are part of the school culture or how we do things around here.

In contrast to norms in school cultures, norms of collaboration are deliberately developed and agreed to. Norms foster the collaboration, build relationships, and help avoid interactions that may derail the learning process.

Typical norms include expectations of behaviors such as (1) listen with an open mind, (2) everyone has a voice, and (3) honor time limits.

Norms could also include anything else that those in the partnership decide is important, like balance advocacy and inquiry; assume positive intentions; and support ideas with data and evidence, rather than personal qualities. Whether the coach and mentor are communicating with one learner or a group, establishing norms for the collaboration will facilitate positive outcomes.

Body and Mind Alignment

Adults have varied ways of processing information. Some write everything down, others do not write anything and just listen intently, while someone else doodles, which helps the person to concentrate. Sharing one's own ways of listening and processing with those in the partnership will advance communication. If members do not share, then when one is doodling, the other may think he is not listening or does not care, when really the opposite is true. Be comfortable in the partnership to seek clarification with queries like, "If this isn't a good time to collaborate, when would be a good time for you?"

If possible, communicating that all are listening with mind and body alignment is ideal. In other words, if one person looks down at his device to check a text while another is speaking, the inference would be disagreement or lack of interest. In contrast, making eye contact and leaning forward is thought to indicate interest and engagement. Some people frown a little or cross their arms when thinking intently or trying to resolve something on their mind. Rather than interpret the deep thinking appearance as negative, invite clarification, "You look like you're thinking something important. Would you share with me?"

Active Listening

Think about a time you had something that was important to you to share, but you got the feeling that the person with whom you were talking did not value the communication like you did. What did the person do that sent you the message of lack of value? Generally, active listening is characterized by the listener seeking clarification and checking for accuracy in understanding, just as in body and mind alignment.

Here is an example. A colleague was overheard saying, "Teachers with high student ratings must be easy!" The listener interpreted that the colleague did not trust the value of the student ratings, so he clarified what he thought by paraphrasing, "Are you saying that teachers with high student ratings are not effective teachers?" After he responded that he did not think the high ratings had anything to do with effectiveness, the listener shared evidence to the contrary, "The teachers I know with high student ratings come to school every day, have student-centered instruction, and often stay after school to give students extra help." Paraphrasing and clarifying with data and evidence, rather than with emotion or personal judgments, are excellent communication strategies to maintain objectivity, authentic communication, and understanding.

Empathizing

As professionals in the practice of education, many are emotionally connected to their mission of improving students' learning. Given their passion for professional work, learners may feel emotions, such as disappointment in themselves or in others. Emotions are natural and when someone in the partnership is expressing emotions related to the work, empathizing with their feelings lets them know that you hear what they are saying and understand. Demeaning or discounting a person's feelings implies that you do not value what he or she feels. A response that discounts a person's feelings might sound like, "It doesn't matter how you feel, just do what you have to do!"

To clarify the difference between empathy and sympathy, consider this common example. An elementary teacher had given students many extra hours of assistance, but the students did not follow-through with their own effort. When the teacher shared his disappointment with his mentor, the response was, "I know you are disappointed in the students' lack of follow-through when you have invested so much time (empathy). What will you do now?" (The mentor refocused the conversation on professional actions). Empathizing is not feeling sorry for a person but is putting yourself in his or her emotional shoes for a moment.

Compare the empathy statement with the one that follows and that is sympathetic. "I am so sorry that the students' efforts don't compare to yours." Which statement will more probably lead to action and which to inaction?

Generative Response

The concept of generative response is so important to the coaching partnership's success that it is revisited and extended in this chapter within the construct of effective communication. When coaches, mentors, and administrators are in a partnership to improve professional practice that is intended to improve student learning outcomes, it is a good idea to lead and respond with open-ended statements that lead the learner to generate potential actions (Puig & Froelich, 2011). Consider a hypothetical classroom visit when you noticed a number of students with their heads on their tables or interacting with their personal devices. In the follow-up reflective discussion, you ask, "What did you notice that the students were doing?" or "Based on what you noticed, what will you do differently next time you teach the same standard?"

Inquiry and deep thinking are other ways to understand generative response. The coach and mentor have, as their purpose, to develop the deep thinking reflective practice as a habit so that the practice continues beyond the relationship. To help build this good habit, coaches and mentors will want to own generative responses that encourage learners' thinking and self-generation of potential solutions and steps. Some good generative responses are: Can you think of other ways to engage students? Did you notice how many students were engaged and how many were not? What role do you think physical proximity plays in student on-task behaviors? Can you think of reasons why students may not engage with the proposed lesson segment?

Co-construction of Strength-based Action

When coaches and mentors begin by focusing on what is going well and the strengths of a learner, they tend to be positive in communications. On the other hand, if colleagues have a deficit focus, then the communication may become clouded with negativity. Deficit thinking creates barriers to building relationships, hearing what is said, and generating and implementing actions to improve practice.

Think about a time you were informed that you had done something incorrectly as an adult. How did you feel? Empowered or deflated? Motivated or demotivated? Receiving negative feedback can create embarrassment and feelings of being ineffective, which may result in withdrawal either psychologically or physically.

Concepts of effective adult communication support the productive coaching and mentoring partnership. All of the elements are most useful when they lead to co-construction of strength-based action and include academic language. Labeling actions and potential actions with academic language makes explicit to the learner that the actions are grounded in research and most likely will be effective.

When the reflective session turns to the action development, co-constructing the action by using the learner's strengths increases the probability that the learner will try to implement the action. Labeling the action helps the learner to know that when he is effective, it is not accidental but purposeful, deliberate, and supported by evidence. In other words, the coach may say, "I have noticed that one of your strengths is the positive relationship you have with your students (high-effect size strategy). Can you think of a way to use this strength to engage more students?" On Figure 1.1, this behavior would be an example of a four, Reflect.

Or, if the learner has a little difficulty in generating a potential action, you can provide an authentic probe, "I noticed that when you moved from the front of the room to each group's table (proximity) and invited students to tell you what they had identified (inquiry), their engagement (thinking about the learning task) increased. This is a real strength. Are there other similar ways you can use proximity and inquiry to increase the frequency (evidence) of engagement?" This behavior on Figure 1.1 is an example of three, Guide.

ACADEMIC LANGUAGE

One of the barriers to improving student achievement is facility with academic language. Within classrooms, teachers may support students' understanding of challenging standards by using language that is easy to access and understand, with the intent of following through with scaffolding students' language to the rigorous academic language of the challenging standard. Unfortunately, time for teaching a standard moves so quickly that teachers may not develop student facility with academic language appropriate to the rigor of the standard. The resulting assessment outcomes often reflect more of the students' academic language proficiency than knowledge of the standard itself.

With the rationale given, academic language is included in this chapter on adult communication. Consistent modeling is an effective language learning instructional strategy. When coaches directly teach general academic language (e.g., write, summarize, scan, connect) and specific academic language to a content area (e.g., inverse, reciprocal, latitude, metaphor) and purposefully model the language, students and adult learners naturally learn the language (Taylor, et al., 2014).

Recently, the authors asked early grades teachers to focus on using the academic language of target standards in their daily conversations with students. When the authors returned to collaborate with these same teachers two weeks later, they shared how surprised they were that the students started using the same language! Teachers no longer said top and bottom number and therefore, students were saying numerator and denominator. Until that time, the teachers had directly taught the concept of fractions but had not directly taught the academic language, because they thought it would be too rigorous for their young learners.

This simple example is shared because when everyone in the coaching partnership (coach, mentor, learner, and administrator) is purposefully deliberate in speaking with academic language on a regular basis, then students will adopt the language. When the administrator consistently models academic language, then the coach and mentor are also more likely to do so. Coaches and mentors are models for teachers, so their consistent use of academic language naturally will lead to the other teachers modeling academic language for students and to student improvement—the learning intention of coaching.

With implementation of rigorous standards, there is an increased expectation of academic language proficiency among students. As an example, the Standards of Mathematical Practice (SMP) are communication standards. These standards reflect the expectation of precision and accuracy in the use of mathematical academic language and in comprehension. The SMP also identify the expectation of precision in oral and written communication related to mathematical problem solving, generation of hypothesis, and support of claims, much like standards in any content do. For students to have proficiency with academic language to the extent that they are successful on the new generation of assessments across content areas, then the adults with whom they interact daily have to directly teach and be models of academic language, both specific and general.

SCENARIO: E-MAIL COMMUNICATION

As a follow-up to collaborative planning with US history, teachers focused on academic language instruction. Hilary, the Columbia High School literacy coach, visited the teachers' classrooms to oversee their ways of implementation. She was disappointed over the inconsistent implementation of the strategies she had shared with them and sent the follow-up e-mail to the group.

> Teachers, I am so disappointed in the lack of implementation of the instructional strategies we discussed last week. When your students do not perform well on the end of course assessment because they do not have academic language, do not blame me. You know where to find me if want my help. Hilary

How do you think the US history teachers will respond?

Think of reasons why Hilary did not see implementation of the strategies she had shared.

How aligned with the purpose of coaching and mentoring is the e-mail?

After you mentally rehearse, jot down the steps you would have taken if you were Hilary.

Edit Hilary's response to reflect effective adult communication, academic language, and strength-based coaching.

TIPS FOR PRODUCTIVE COMMUNICATION

Learner

Learners are encouraged to invite coaching, mentoring, and administrator support. Sometimes learners wait for someone else to initiate the support and then, the time of need will have passed. Few teachers ask for assistance (Mangin & Dunsmore, 2015). Be the one to ask your coach, mentor, or administrator to visit your classroom and reflect with you on one specific professional action you identify as an improvement goal. Focus on one small item, like waiting for students to think prior to asking for individuals to respond. After you have reflected with the coach or mentor, let him or her know what she said or did that was helpful, such as "When you act like you have confidence in me, it helps me to believe I can be an effective teacher" or "When you asked me to think about the evidence, it seemed like I could also measure change in the evidence and success became doable."

Do not be shy to ask for the administrator's time and thinking. The administrator wants you to be an effective teacher and to have the resources, time, and support needed.

Coach and Mentor

To be effective, coaches and mentors must be purposeful and deliberate in their communications and actions. Planning the conversation and reflection, using academic language, and being armed with research on effective instruction are all as important for you as instructional planning is for teachers.

In a study of first year science and mathematics teachers and their mentors, several things which coaches and mentors will want to keep in mind emerged. Learners want time with coaches and mentors, even if they do not ask for it. The novice teachers found that assisting with lesson planning, allowing them to visit the mentor's class, and offering resources was helpful. One said the most helpful action was "just checking in to see how I'm doing." Also, they want to hear communication framed in positive language and positive dispositions related to students, schools, and education. Specifically, one first year science teacher, rated as highly effective by her principal, said "Focus on strategies, you hear a lot of complaining, this is okay, but don't forget a solution is possible. This is what my mentor did that helped me a lot; gave me solutions and examples of solutions." Similarly, a mathematics teacher voiced, "Always stay positive and most important sit back and listen; sometimes that is all we need" (Karcinski, 2015).

Consistent modeling of adult communication strategies and academic language will help learners adopt the same practices. The demonstration of mutual respect builds the professional relationship among all who are in the partnership. Modeling of the development of productive relationships, academic language, and effective communication will enable the learner to adopt the same professional practices and transfer these to their instruction and interactions with students.

Arm yourself with stems for generative responses as modeled in chapter 3 and in this chapter. Keep in mind that the learner needs to know what worked and why, so that effective practice can be repeated. Learners need to know what did not work and how it might work better. The coaching and mentoring skill needed is to help the learner generate these thoughts and for you to label them for clear understanding and consistent practice to automaticity.

Let the learner make the judgment, not you. Maintain communication consistent with the facilitator of the learning role, rather than with the role of judge or evaluator. Coaches and mentors facilitate individual or group change (Ippolito, 2010).

Find resources that are easy to access and support the coaching and mentoring process. Two resources, *Why Didn't I Learn this in College* (Rutherford, 2009) and *The 21st Century Mentor's Handbook* (Rutherford, 2008), are coordinated. The learner's text is referenced in the mentor and coach's text so that both do not have to be in the same location to have discussions. Also, adopting texts for the coaching and mentoring partnerships assists in the development of common language and expectations.

Remember that both mentors and coaches learn through a productive partnership. Evidence from coaches and mentors is a reminder that the model is a learning partnership: "I was reminded of strategies through our conversations" and "Planning with my mentee helped me to be more explicit in my teaching" (Karcinski, 2015). The partnership is a win-win-win relationship.

Administrator

Administrators are wise to remember that they set the bar for everything, but most importantly for expectations and communication. How the administrators communicate, either with general, vague, or negative language or with precise and positive language will set the expectation for all adults in the setting. Be a model of positive and effective adult communication strategies!

Academic language was addressed in this chapter as a critical component in advancing student achievement in any learning environment. If administrators believe in the important role of academic language in increasing student achievement, then their purposeful and deliberate use of specific academic language will be a model for others to follow. For instance, in a meeting you can think aloud, "As I was reflecting on yesterday's class visits, I thought about the student engagement evidence I saw and heard. Marisol was using her device to find zebra fish and their offspring. With obvious excitement she shared with other students her observation analysis."

Studies that analyzed the trust that teachers and staff have with administrators conclude that communication is the most powerful trust builder (Arneson, 2012). Invite communication not by saying, "Drop by, I have an open door policy" but by going to teachers and coaches without an appointment just to listen to them, not to tell them anything. Invitations to others to share perspectives and feedback build the relationship. Specifically, invite thinking on what you can do to support coach, mentor, and learner-enhanced effectiveness. Listen!

While the administrator's role includes making judgments and evaluating others, communication skill may determine the extent to which broad-scale improvement of learning takes place. When combined with skillful communication, judgments and evaluations will have a better chance of acceptance and of stimulating continued improvement in effectiveness to facilitate school-wide or district-wide change (Ippolito, 2010).

COMMUNICATIVE REFLECTIVE PRACTICE

Reflection is a recommended professional practice for all those involved in the partnership. Review the Coaching System Planning Tool in Appendix A and generate your next steps for the Academic Language and Communication rows.

Learner

Learners are responsible for productive coaching and mentoring partnerships. Practice the following stems to invite positive communication and design your own to use for improved communication with coaches, mentors, and administrators.

- I wonder if you would have time to . . . ?
- I think if I could visit a classroom when a teacher is . . .
- Would you assist me in planning for teaching . . . standard? When could we co-plan?
- Would it be possible for me to attend . . . professional learning offered by . . . ?

Coach and Mentor

This chapter has focused on effective adult communication and developing the learner's reflective practice. Developing your own fluency in these strategies and in reflective practice takes time. Think about stems to help you reflect on your own professional practice.

- The learner generated his own solution when I . . .
- When I . . . learners request more time with me.

- When I . . . learners do not ask for my assistance.
- Evidence that my coaching and mentoring is changing teacher effectiveness is . . .
- Evidence that administrators understand the coaching partnership include . . .

Practice the following stems to model positive communication and design your own reflective practice for improved mentoring and coaching communication.

- What did you notice when . . . ?
- Think about a time when . . .
- What are some strategies that have worked for you in the past? What did you do (action) that led to success?
- When would you like to co-plan for . . . ?
- What do you think about . . . ?
- When lessons are less effective than others, what do you do differently?

Administrator

Administrators should be models for communication strategies that they would like to see coaches, mentors, and teachers implement. Practice the following stems to model positive communication and to invite coaching and mentoring.

- I wonder if you would assist me in planning . . . ?
- What is the best part about . . . ?
- How can I improve . . . ?
- What resources do you need to achieve your professional goals?
- How can I support the productive coach, mentor, and learner partnership?

DEFINITIONS

Academic language   Language that is essential for success in school and on assessments. General academic language includes vocabulary that transcends content and is important for independent success (e.g., analyze, chronological order, contrast, summary). Discipline-specific academic language is essential for success in a particular content area or course (e.g., reciprocal, respiratory system, geography, literary elements).

Active listening	Body and language alignment that demonstrates attention to the speaker, and concern for understanding and shared meaning.
Co-construct	Develop together for mutual ownership and to enhance the quality of the implementation.
Empathy	Responsiveness that shows compassion and or identification with feelings.
Fluency	Anything done with appropriate rate and accuracy.
Generative response	Encourages thinking and generates ownership of the solution or next step.
Strength-based	Communication that emphasizes strengths of the learner, rather than deficits. It communicates empowerment and confidence in the learner.

RESOURCES

Arneson, S. (2012). *Communicate and Motivate: The School Leader's Guide to Effective Communication*. Eye on Education.

Costa, A. L. & Garmston, R. J. (1994). *Cognitive Coaching: A Foundation for Renaissance in Schools*. Norwood, MA: Christopher-Gordon.

Ippolito, J. (2010). Three Ways that Literacy Coaches Balance Responsive and Directive Relationships with Teachers. *Elementary School Journal. 3*: 164–90.

Johnson, J. (2011). *You Can't Do it Alone: A Communications and Engagement Manual for School Leaders*. Lanham, MD: Rowman & Littlefield Education.

Knight, J. (Editor). (2009). *Coaching Approaches and Perspectives*. Thousand Oaks, CA: Corwin Press; Reston, VA: NASSP.

Puig, E. A. & Froelich, K. S. (2011). *The Literacy Coach: Guiding in the Right Direction* (2nd edition). Boston: Allyn & Bacon Publishers.

Rutherford, P. (2008). *21st Century Mentor's Handbook: Creating a Culture of Learning*. Alexandria, VA: Just Ask Publications.

Rutherford, P. (2009). *Why Didn't I Learn this in College*. Alexandria, VA: Just Ask Publications.

Chapter 6

Coaching Process

Previous chapters highlighted the significance of well-defined roles, generative thinking, relationships, and effective communication in creating the conditions for productive coaching partnerships. These important elements together contribute to the coaching and mentoring partnership system. Having a defined coaching and mentoring process, including actions and steps, is fundamental to achieving improved teaching and learning outcomes. This chapter will explore how to establish a well-defined process for coaching and mentoring so that roles, generative thinking, relationships, and communication support the coaching process.

In a review of the literature, Gallucci, Lare, Yoon, and Boatright (2010) found common elements within the coaching process. These instructional coaching elements are reflected in this text and in the cyclical nature of the coaching process. Instructional coaching is:

- content based (e.g., mathematics coaching or literacy coaching) and supports teachers in meeting school and/or school district goals;
- job-embedded and includes observations of teaching, lesson modeling, and preconferences and postconferences;
- with teachers, identifies modes for teacher learning, models teaching, gathers data, and engages teachers in dialogue;
- that which requires communication skills, building relationships, managing change, and leading professional learning; and
- that which requires ongoing learning on the part of the coach.

There are coaching models that address these elements. Common to most models is a cyclical, recursive structure that is centered on adult and student learning. The cyclical process includes a research base, modeling,

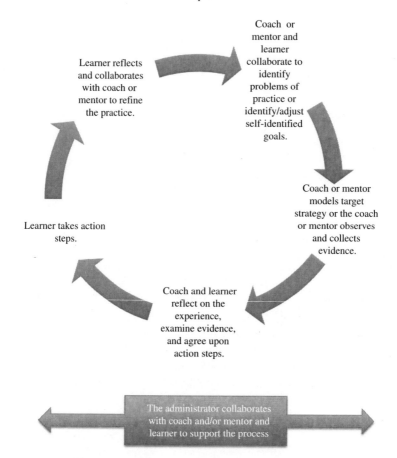

Coach or mentor and learner collaborate to identify problems of practice or identify/adjust self-identified goals.

Learner reflects and collaborates with coach or mentor to refine the practice.

Coach or mentor models target strategy or the coach or mentor observes and collects evidence.

Learner takes action steps.

Coach and learner reflect on the experience, examine evidence, and agree upon action steps.

The administrator collaborates with coach and/or mentor and learner to support the process

Figure 6.1   Coaching Partnership Process Model. *Source*: Rosemarye T. Taylor & Carol Chanter.

observation, data and evidence collection, practice, feedback, reflection, and collaboration (National Center on Quality Teaching and Learning, 2014). The authors support a student-centered and learner-driven approach to coaching, as illustrated in Figure 6.1.

INDIVIDUAL COACHING

In the coaching partnership process model, the teacher and coach or mentor are actively involved in collaborative inquiry. They begin with generative thinking to identify a goal or problem of practice to be solved or improved upon. Problems of practice may be student centered or learner centered.

For example, the learner may inquire about how students might generate more questions or how the learner might make more explicit connections between the content and students' lives. A coach of instructional coaches may focus on how a coach may be reflective instead of being directive. Similarly, the administrator might examine testing data and identify multiplication and division of whole numbers and fractions as a school-wide problem of practice.

Once the problem of practice is self-identified and a self-directed learning goal agreed upon, the coach or mentor may model a target strategy, co-teach a strategy, or invite the learner to view a model on an accessible site. Another option is for the learner, coach, or mentor to observe a peer and collect evidence related to the identified problem of practice.

Following the experience, the coach or mentor and learner reflect on the experience, examine evidence, and agree upon action steps. The learner then applies the agreed-upon action steps. This application of action steps may take place immediately or within a week or two of the coaching session. Finally, the learner reflects and collaborates with the coach or mentor to refine the practice, and the cycle begins again with refinement of the same practice or with the identification of a new problem of practice and self-directed learning goal.

This recursive inquiry-based process assures that the coach or mentor and learner are engaged in trying new strategies, gathering and analyzing evidence, reflecting, providing feedback, and receiving feedback. Most importantly, the coach or mentor and learner are learning together to solve problems of practice and improve student learning outcomes. By owning the problem of practice, self-directed learning goal, and improvements, motivation for self-directed learning is fostered.

GROUP-BASED COACHING FOR SCHOOL-WIDE OR SCHOOL DISTRICT-WIDE IMPROVEMENT

Sometimes the number of available coaches and allocated time may limit the capacity for individual coaching of teachers. The authors support the use of the same coaching process model for both group coaching for school-wide and/or system-wide improvement and for individual learner coaching focused on individual self-identified goals. For group-based coaching, the process will have a sequence similar to individual coaching.

1. In collaboration with the administrator, the coach works with teams or job-alike groups to identify a school-wide or team common problem of practice that leads to a team learning goal.

2. Once the learning goal is identified, the coach models or provides for modeling of the target strategy for the entire group or team. This might take place in a virtual classroom, simulated classroom session with the adults taking on the role of the students, or within an actual classroom. Adults observe instruction of students and collect evidence.
3. The coach and learners debrief and reflect on the experience, examine evidence, and agree on team action steps and a timeline for completion.
4. Learners then take the agreed-upon action steps to their job-embedded settings.
5. The learners and coach meet together to analyze evidence, reflect on the experiences, and agree upon next steps for refinement, or identify a new problem of practice and set a new learning goal.
6. The coaching process continues.

Some coaching models or protocols focus solely on individual teacher improvement. The authors support a blended approach that includes individual and group coaching. Group coaching focuses on instructional or professional goals for school-wide and/or system-wide change. Large-scale improvement can be achieved by proportioning the coach's time to support individual teachers as well as by regularly scheduling group-coaching sessions focused on school-wide and/or system-wide instructional goals. Examples of system-wide or school-wide goals may be to improve academic language instruction or to incorporate formative assessments.

The same concept of large-scale coaching and mentoring applies to coaching of the mentors and coaches, administrators, and other professionals in the school and school district. There will be overlap among the school-wide, school district-wide coaching with individual learning goals. These overlaps provide connections, thus strengthening the coaching partnership system. Figure 6.2 illustrates this blended process.

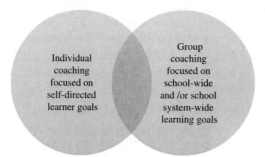

Figure 6.2   Blended Model for Individual and Group Coaching. *Source*: Rosemarye T. Taylor & Carol Chanter.

COACHING MODES

In addition to individual- and group-based coaching, there are blended ways to focus and format the delivery of coaching. The choices made depend on the school or school district structure, coaching capacity, coaching goals, and learner needs. Schools and school district leaders should consider if the coaching will be delivered to individual learners, groups, or to a combination of both.

In addition, leaders will want to decide if coaching concentrates on building capacities to support a curriculum initiative or instructional strategy, individual learning goals, school-wide and/or school district-wide improvement, or a combination. For example, school district-level coaches might focus on building the expertise of school-based coaches to model a specific strategy like close reading, or an external coach may concentrate on building school district capacity to sustain a curriculum implementation.

Even when a school-wide or school district-wide coaching focus has been identified, coaches will quickly uncover additional individual learner needs. Common examples include improving teacher-student relationships, managing the learning environment, building content knowledge, or implementing curriculum. Based on the focus areas, some combinations of individual and group-based coaching will most likely provide the best solution to achieve the coaching goals.

Defining the coaching delivery modes in a time-specific manner will help determine the frequency and intensity of the coaching. If coaching capacity is constrained by the number of coaches or allocated time, then the school district-wide focus for learning could be addressed within group coaching. Predictable interval sessions, like monthly group coaching may take place, while individual teacher needs could be addressed within classrooms more frequently.

Also, depending on learner preferences, needs, and available resources, the coaching process may be enhanced and blended with other types of professional learning opportunities, including workshops, videos, webinars, simulations, online modules, book studies, action research, and lesson study. Collaborative planning, professional learning communities, data/evidence study, and peer modeling can also produce effective professional learning (Speir, 2015; Taylor & Gordon, 2014; Taylor, et al., 2013; Moxley & Taylor, 2006). Table 6.1 provides examples of how the coaching delivery mode and process might be scheduled.

Whether with individuals, groups, or a combination of both, the process encompasses the components necessary to create an effective coaching system. Through the methods of identifying the problem(s) of practice, selecting a learning goal, and agreeing upon schedules and delivery modes, the process

Table 6.1   Sample Coaching and Mentoring Modes, Learners, Processes, and Schedules

Mode	Learner	Process and Schedule
Individual	Self-identified Coach or mentor-identified Administrator-identified	Ongoing inquiry, reflection, and discussion. Identify and remedy problems of practice.
Group	Job-alike groups led by coach, administrator, teacher, or mentor	Monthly group coaching session during common planning time
Webinar	School-level mathematics coaches led by school district mathematics coach	Monthly web-based learning opportunity. Bimonthly face-to-face school district session
Mixed Reality	School-level or school district–level administrators led by administrator coach	Monthly virtual learning Quarterly face-to-face school or district-wide professional learning
Professional Learning Community (PLC)	Middle school science teachers led by science coach	Monthly PLC meeting Book study Quarterly individual coaching on PLC-selected action steps

Source: Rosemarye T. Taylor & Carol Chanter.

begins. By incorporating action steps, gathering and analyzing evidence, and reflecting on the process, measurable outcomes can be determined.

Instructional leadership to create a coaching culture for professional learning is required (Annenberg Report on Instructional Coaching, n.d.). Administrators, coaches, mentors, and learners may also find *Coaching Approaches and Perspectives*, edited by Jim Knight (2009), offers a wealth of information on coaching processes and modes.

SCENARIO: PROFESSIONAL LEARNING AND THE COACHING PARTNERSHIP PROCESS

At Jefferson Middle School, Mr. Johnson, the principal, and Ms. Jascinski, the coach, met in July before the school year began, to scope out the coaching plan for the year. Both were in a hurry to get the plan written so that Mr. Johnson could submit it to the superintendent. Ms. Jascinski did not want to be at school since her professional contract did not start until mid-August.

Since the state assessment was changing this year, they decided upon a series of monthly after-school professional learning sessions to address popular topics which they thought were considered best practices: differentiating instruction, thinking strategies, engaging and motivating students, and wait time. Ms. Jascinksi let her administrator, Mr. Johnson, know that because of the extra time she would have to spend preparing for each session, in addition to her regular duties of managing the school book room, monitoring students' arrival, and supporting twelve new teachers, she would not have much time left for individual teacher follow-up. Mr. Johnson agreed that her time was stretched, but thought that the professional learning sessions were important to prepare the teachers and students for the new assessments. He added, "Who could argue with the topics anyway?"

The year began and the teachers dutifully attended the monthly professional learning sessions. The feedback on the sessions was very positive; however, Mr. Johnson could not understand why during his weekly walkthroughs he rarely saw any of the practices from the sessions taking place in the classrooms. (For more information on walkthroughs, see chapter 7.)

Down the street at Robinson High School, Mrs. Cline, the school principal and Mr. Ernst, the school instructional coach, had a similar meeting in the summer. Their professional learning plan for the year was much different than that at Jefferson Middle School. To plan for professional learning, Mrs. Cline and Mr. Ernst analyzed the data from the previous year's assessments, reviewed the teachers' instructional practices outcomes from walkthroughs, and noted student demographic variables as evidence to set goals. Mrs. Cline knew that review of at least three data or evidence sources should be considered in making such important decisions to avoid invalid conclusions.

Their data analysis revealed that about 20 percent of the students did not complete the writing portion of the accountability assessment. They hypothesized that students ran out of time or stamina to complete this portion of the assessment, which resulted in an overall decline in school scores. They also noticed that students scored consistently low in vocabulary and summarization. In addition, there were great differences among student scores of teachers who taught similar courses with similar student demographic groups.

Review of the patterns of instructional practices documented for the previous year reminded Mrs. Cline and Mr. Ernest that the teachers seemed to be assigning writing, instead of teaching and modeling the writing expectations. They also noted lack of explicit feedback provided to students on written work, which may have led to the lack of improvement in writing and completion of that portion of the assessment.

As they reflected on the data and evidence, they inferred that the writing scores as a problem of practice may have been exacerbated by the lack of academic language instruction and practice in summarization. The writing assessment score was dependent upon facility with science and social studies academic language and expertise in writing summaries. Based on the data and evidence, the agreed-upon plan was a blended approach to professional learning for the year. For whole-school face-to-face meetings, they would dedicate one after-school session per quarter to non-negotiable strategies:

- research-based vocabulary routines and academic language instruction,
- writing routines for building stamina and text analysis,
- strategies for teaching summarization, and
- research-based feedback.

In addition, they identified mentor teachers in each content area, who exemplified effective instructional practices and improved achievement. The plan included release time for the mentor/teachers to provide in-classroom support on non-negotiable strategies to their team members. Time and resources for mentors to support self-identified learning goals of individuals were also provided. The mentor teachers would also participate in monthly webinars and quarterly mentor meetings led by the instructional coach to review the coaching process and research-based practices, and to examine evidence of improved student learning for writing, academic language, summarization, and feedback. Monies were provided for quarterly release time for content area teachers to observe instruction in the mentor teacher's classroom. The coach and teachers collaboratively would develop observation protocols to focus the observations on target instructional strategies and evidence of student learning. Finally, the instructional coach, along with the mentor teachers, would meet monthly with content area teams for a group coaching session to support the focus areas and to build mentors' expertise in the coaching process.

The year began, and during the opening staff meeting, Mrs. Cline led the teachers through a data analysis of last year's test scores. Teachers identified the same areas of concern that Mrs. Cline and Mr. Ernst had discovered. Mrs. Cline then shared the plan and invited feedback. Mr. Ernst led their identification of problems of practice. Teachers were encouraged to sign up for mentor coaching sessions if they would like support in improving their self-identified problems of practice and learning goal.

Reflect for a moment on the scenarios. Hypothesize why Mr. Johnson did not observe implementation of strategies targeted in the professional learning sessions during classroom walkthroughs. Which school reflects a culture of coaching and professional learning? What evidence supports your thinking? If you were the coach at Jefferson Middle School, what would you have said or what actions you would have taken to help Mr. Johnson consider refinements for the use of Ms. Jascinski's coaching time?

TIPS FOR A PRODUCTIVE COACHING PARTNERSHIP

Learner

Being knowledgeable about your learning preferences can help shape modes for coaching and guide initial discussions with your coach or mentor. Individual preferences for learning may include those that are technology supported and allow for flexibility in location (bug-in-the-ear or virtual). Maybe your preference is to be face-to-face. Perhaps you like individual or group coaching supported by readings, video, audio, or other text and digital resources. Resources such as the online VARK Questionnaire provide a quick way to learn more about personal learning preferences: http://vark-learn.com/the-vark-questionnaire/.

In addition to being cognizant of your preferred learning modes, identifying a problem of practice that you are passionate to improve upon is an engaging way to begin the inquiry-based coaching process. Identifying a problem of practice simply means that you gather data and evidence (student grades, test scores, observations, student work, etc.) to identify a professional practice upon which you would like to improve. If you improved on the professional practice, student learning would also improve. The Teaching Channel offers an exemplary video that models how teachers can practice gathering evidence related to problems of practice. At this site, you can also find guiding questions for determining individual problems of practice: https://www.teachingchannel.org/videos/problem-of-practice.

Coach and Mentor

The coach or mentor is an expert in facilitating the coaching process. Whether coaching groups or individuals, the coach takes learners through the steps of identifying a problem of practice, setting learning goals, learning, gathering, and analyzing evidence, practicing new learning, reflecting, and refining practice. This sophisticated skill of moving adult learners along a continuum of instructional expertise is the heart and soul of the coaching role.

By placing professional inquiry at the center of the coaching process, coaches and mentors will naturally continue to improve their practice. Their role development includes professional growth, generative thinking, communication, and relationship building. As coaches and mentors refine the inquiry-based coaching process, they create an environment for change. Coaches and mentors may find the resource, *The Adaptive School: A Sourcebook for Developing Collaborative Groups, 2nd Edition* (Garmston & Wellman, 2013), helpful in defining coaching and mentoring problems and identifying strategies to solve them. This resource also provides a useful CD-ROM containing 150 facilitation strategies.

It is no surprise to coaches and mentors that inquiry, analysis of data and evidence, and reflection work hand in hand. In addition to practicing inquiry, coaches and mentors are instruments of change when they become experts in understanding, practicing, and facilitating data/evidence analysis-based reflection.

Being a change agent means helping others understand how reflection improves professional practice. When coaches and mentors model reflection and make the steps of reflection explicit, learners are better able to apply their newly discovered insights to instruction and professional practice. This position is supported by the Interstate Teacher Assessment and Support Consortium (InTASC) Model Core Teaching Standards and Learning Progressions for Teachers 1.0 (2014). Specifically, Standards 9a, 9b, 9d, 9k, 9n, and 10t identify that the teacher

> actively seeks professional, community, and technological resources, within and outside the school, as supports for analysis, reflection, and problem-solving and based on *reflection* and other sources of feedback, the teacher takes responsibility for his/her self-assessment of practice and ongoing professional learning by seeking out and participating in professional learning experiences to address identified needs and areas of professional interest. (p. 42)

When coaches and mentors support the practice of reflection, they are helping teachers to more fully address related professional standards and improve practice. Coaches and mentors may find the resource, *Examining and Facilitating Reflection to Improve Professional Practice* (Harris, et al., 2010), useful in developing expertise in the practice of reflection.

Administrator

Administrators have the task of creating and supporting a coaching culture that embraces the coaching process as a means to improve instructional practice. As highlighted in the scenario, a coaching culture does not exist just because the school or individuals have a professional learning plan. For the coaching process to be part of the culture, it must be explicitly and purposely developed and reinforced. Administrators should model inquiry and reflection by participating in the coaching process. Rewarding participation will encourage others to participate.

Resources, such as *Cognitive Coaching: Weaving Threads of Learning and Change Into The Culture of an Organization* (Ellison & Hayes, 2013), can provide insight into how to enculturate coaching and build trust in the process. Successful administrators stay the course of supporting the implementation of the coaching partnership process.

REFLECTIVE PRACTICE TO ASSURE THE COACHING PARTNERSHIP PROCESS

The coaching process includes elements that improve teacher effectiveness and student learning (Knight, et al., 2015). To gain the greatest benefit from the coaching process, learners, coaches and mentors, and administrators should maintain a curious, metacognitive, and reflective state of mind. Review Appendix A, rows titled Data and Evidence and Assessment, and think about your next steps.

As you reflect on the coaching process outlined in this chapter, think about how to identify the problem of practice, goal, or plan for improvement. Refer to Figure 6.1 to analyze how responsibilities will be shared. Collaborate to implement the process. Use the following questions to help frame a discussion on the basis of your reflection.

- What professional learning and tools will be needed to help learners identify problems of practice and set learning goals?
- What types of data or evidence will be collected and utilized to demonstrate progress on the learning goals?
- What coaching modes will best meet the needs of your team (learners, coaches, mentors, and administrators)?
- What observation and/or reflection tools might learners and coaches find useful when observing instruction and/or modeled strategies?
- How will time be allocated and managed to support the coaching partnership process?

When talking about corporate coaching, John Russell, managing director, Harley-Davidson Europe Ltd. (2011), stated, "I never cease to be amazed at the power of the coaching process to draw out the skills or talent that was previously hidden within an individual, and which invariably finds a way to solve a problem previously thought unsolvable." Even though Mr. Russell was referencing corporate coaching, the process of coaching adults in education has the same power to draw out hidden skills and talents.

Although learners may like their coach or mentor, it is not the coach or mentor they should trust most but the process. The process of collaboratively identifying data- or evidence-based problems of practice, setting learning goals, taking action, reflecting, and adjusting professional practices is the course to facilitate. In return, this process allows learners, coaches, mentors, and administrators to become more reflective, effective leaders and learners. It is the coaching process powered by open-ended questions and reflection that can transform thinking from closed to generative. Leverage the coaching process to move toward generative thinking that will positively impact student learning outcomes.

DEFINITIONS

Adult Learning	How adults learn which emphasizes the value of the process of learning and uses approaches that are problem based and collaborative, rather than didactic. Emphasizes equality between the coach or mentor and the learner.
Coaching Mode	The timeframe, structure (groups or individuals) and method for delivering job-embedded professional learning though coaching.
Coaching Process	A series of steps and actions for learners, coaches and mentors, and administrators that enable learners to improve effectiveness resulting in improved student learning.
Inquiry	The act of investigating or of seeking information with open-ended questions such as, What do you think? What did you notice?
Job-embedded	The location of professional learning and the direct connection between a learner's work and the professional learning and/or coaching received.
Problem of Practice	Data or evidence-based need for improvement that leads to the self-identified learning goal.

RESOURCES

Ellison, J. L. & Hayes, C. (2013). *Cognitive Coaching: Weaving Threads of Learning and Change into the Culture of an Organization.* Lanham, MD: Rowman & Littlefield, Education Division.

Ellison, J. L. & Hayes, C. (2013). *Effective School Leadership: Developing Principals Through Cognitive Coaching.* Lanham, MD: Rowman & Littlefield, Education Division.

Garmston, R. J. & Wellman, B. M. (2013). *The Adaptive School: A Sourcebook for Developing Collaborative Groups* (2nd edition). Lanham, MD: Rowman & Littlefield, Education Division.

Harris, A. S., Bruster, B. Peterson, B., & Shutt, T. (2010). *Examining and Facilitating Reflection to Improve Professional Practice*. Lanham, MD: Rowman & Littlefield, Education Division.

Knight, J. (Editor). (2009). *Coaching: Approaches and Perspectives*. Thousand Oaks, CA: Corwin Press.

The Teaching Channel (Producer). (2015, July 4). Thinking Critically About Practice [Video file]. Retrieved from https://www.teachingchannel.org/videos/problem-of-practice.

VARK Learn Limited (Producer). (2015, July 4). The VARK questionnaire: How do I learn best [Online questionnaire]. Retrieved from http://vark-learn.com/the-vark-questionnaire/.

Chapter 7

Expert Practitioners

In the previous chapters, the essential components of a productive coaching partnership were addressed. Chapter 1 began by identifying that pedagogy and content expertise are both essential—not one or the other—to be an effective teacher. Effective or effectiveness was defined as the stable relationship between professional actions and student learning (Konstantopoulous, 2014). Another area that needs to be at the forefront of the partnership is the continual development of everyone's expertise.

Continuous development of expertise is grounded in the belief that success should not be accidental but deliberate with knowledge of how certain professional behaviors and strategies work better than others. With this kind of knowledge, high-impact professional behaviors can be repeated and professional fluency developed. As repeated practice with generative coaching and feedback (as noted in chapters 3 and 5) is experienced, efficiency of the practice will improve until overlearning or automaticity occurs. Overlearning or automaticity results in fluency (appropriate rate and accuracy). This means that the high-impact behaviors become the individual's professional norm.

Purposeful and deliberate successful professional practice results in self-efficacy by teachers, coaches, mentors, and administrators. Self-efficacy is the belief that our values and actions change student learning outcomes. To support the development of self-efficacy, expertise is to be continually developed. This chapter addresses the issue of deepening the expertise in content knowledge and pedagogy to increase effectiveness of teachers, coaches, mentors, and administrators.

Planned development of knowledge and skills to support self-development and that of others is capacity building, as defined in chapter 2. As each individual's expertise and knowledge deepens, the coach, mentor, and administrators will lead with more effectiveness. Thus, the capacity of the school, school district, or organization is expanded to improve student learning outcomes.

As happens in any dynamic organization, faculty and administrators will transition to other work locations. Organizations with a deliberate focus on continuous capacity building assure that student learning outcomes are not negatively impacted when these professional transitions occur. Learning outcomes are not dependent on only a few, as the capacity has been continuously developed with deepening expertise to support and lead new members.

RESEARCH-BASED ACCESSIBLE RESOURCES

As a basis for assuring evidence-based or research-based instructional and leadership practice, readers should have resources that are easy to use and promote consistency in practice. For broad use, resources have to be easily understood to maximize their potential in improving effectiveness. Emphasis is on accessibility. Think about resources beyond texts, such as those of nonprofit organizations, like AmeriCorps, Teacher Corps, and the local educator preparation institution.

Examples listed in the resource section of this chapter include the works of John Hattie (2009, 2012), which are accessible for deepening understanding of research-based instructional and leadership behaviors. Two of the author's texts to consider are *Improving Reading, Writing, and Content Learning* (Taylor, 2007) and *Leading, Teaching Learning the Common Core Standards: Rigorous Expectations for All Students* (Taylor, et al., 2014). These accessible resources are intended to create mental models through authentic examples to assist with practical implementation of research-based instruction and leadership. Pragmatic resources assist in refining skills for supporting learners in displacing ineffective practice with more effective practice, resulting in both individual and whole-school improvement.

Effect Size Research

Hattie (2009, 2012) shares findings from thousands of studies that were rigorously examined to conclude that an effect size of $d = 0.40$ is average and the hinge point for considering a practice to impact student learning. Effect size refers to the probability that a specific professional behavior will improve learning. Coaches, mentors, and administrators may want to identify practices with effect sizes greater than $d = 0.40$ to target for implementation. Those with lower effect sizes may be targeted for further in-context examination to determine how to adjust for greater effects or to eliminate.

After some study and discussion on instructional practices and related effect sizes, Kristin, an instructional coach in a high-needs middle school, shared that in her school many low-effect size strategies were regularly used. She noted that reciprocal teaching has a high-effect size of $d = 0.74$ and asked, "Why would we use other instructional strategies when we see the high-effect size for reciprocal teaching?" She followed with, "That effect size even takes into account those who implemented reciprocal teaching incorrectly, pulling the effect size down. Imagine how much the students would learn if we implemented reciprocal teaching with fidelity!" As an exemplary coach, Kristin was analyzing and thinking of demonstrating her effectiveness.

Effect size alone is not enough to make a decision to use a practice or not to use a practice. Context is an important consideration that includes the community expectations, school district expectations, priorities, other related knowledge, and cultural norms.

For example, homework has a low-effect size when used with elementary school students and contrasts with a higher effect size when used with secondary school students. Take a moment to hypothesize reasons why homework might not be as effective to improve student learning in early grades as in middle or high school. Some possible reasons may be:

- No one was at home to help the elementary students with the homework;
- The students did not clearly understand the content, concept, or skills before leaving school and practiced incorrectly; or
- The teacher assigned on-grade level reading homework as a way to introduce a new chapter.

Any of the reasons noted make sense. Homework is independent practice (low teacher support) and students should demonstrate at least 90 percent accuracy with content, concepts, or skills before moving to independent practice. If a student does not read independently on the level of the text assigned, how can the student read by himself and comprehend to be prepared for the next day's class? In either of these situations, most likely the young student will become frustrated and not complete the homework or will practice incorrectly, unless there is a caregiver present who assists with the reading and comprehension.

These hypotheses are based on research beyond that of the effect size of homework. Research considered includes literacy learning and how to scaffold students to successfully move from direct instruction (high teacher support) to guided practice (moderate teacher support) to independent practice (low teacher support), and to mastery. As an added note, assessment should follow demonstration of success in independent practice and mastery.

On the other hand, think about this alternate process for instructional decision-making. The research on homework is discussed in a collaborative professional group of coaches, mentors, administrators, and teachers. Results of the discussion include the identification of research-based ways to assure that homework in early grades will be more effective. Then, teachers implement the criteria that they believe will support effective homework. Criteria may include:

- Assuring 90 percent accuracy independently prior to students going home to practice;
- Assuring that the homework will not require a knowledgeable caregiver to provide assistance;
- Replacing on-grade-level independent reading with visual prereading; or
- Reading that is on the student's independent reading level.

After implementation, the teachers might gather evidences of effective homework (e.g., completion rates or increased demonstration of understanding) during the next class session. These evidences would help the teachers, coaches, mentors, and administrators to collaboratively determine if the altered homework practice improved student learning.

Following their analysis, the collaborative team may choose to provide homework assistance before school, during school, and after school for students who need support. Discussion of the professional behaviors that are needed will conclude with those actions needed to assure improvement.

The intention of this homework example is to share that effect size is important, but it alone may not provide enough evidence upon which to make a decision about professional practice. Three pieces of evidence are recommended to inform any decision (e.g., students do not complete homework or do it incorrectly, parents do not or cannot assist, students are not making acceptable progress on mastering standards). And yet, effect sizes can be a leverage to discover how to improve professional practice.

By accessing resources, like those recommended in this text, you can develop a deeper understanding of the research or explanation that led to the effect size. When understanding of the research is followed by deep thinking, analysis, and solution-seeking then meaningful conclusions and informed actions will be identified. Everyone in the coaching partnership will be empowered with research, evidence, and positive results.

Analysis as described, coupled with understanding your own context, is important. With the example of homework, you may find communities in which the families want homework because they associate homework with their own experiences as learners. The important point is not whether to have homework or not as part of student practice but to have fidelity in homework practice aligned with the research on independent practice.

Educator Preparation Institutions

Other resources to consider for developing expertise may be the local college, university, educator preparation institution, or professional learning organization. There are many professionals who have deep content and pedagogical expertise. Developing substantive partnerships with these experts for just-in-time professional learning or access at the point of need can be helpful. Generally, university faculties welcome the opportunity to partner with educators, particularly if they may collect data on results and share with others your successful practices.

One example of partnering with a university expert took place during an urban school district's lesson study facilitation. Lesson study is a collaborative process in which several teachers and a knowledgeable other (outside expert) make up a lesson study research team, led by a facilitator. In the coaching partnership, the lesson study facilitator may be the coach, mentor, administrator, teacher leader, or any other professional who is skilled in inquiry and reflective practice.

The lesson study research team collaborates to design a standards-based lesson that is taught by one of the members. The rest observe the lesson implementation, gather observational evidence of student learning, and discuss how to make the lesson more effective on the basis of the evidence (Lewis & Hurd, 2011). The process is repeated with another lesson study research team member implementing the revised lesson. The purpose of the collaborative cyclical lesson study process is to improve the teachers' expertise through application of research and reflective practice; it is not to have a perfect lesson (Lewis & Hurd, 2011).

In implementation of a lesson study with mathematics teachers, coaches and mentors, the school district facilitator invited a university mathematics educator to participate as a knowledgeable other or expert. During the lesson study, the mathematics educator demonstrated how to clarify specific mathematical misconceptions effectively. The lesson study research team had not thought of misconceptions in the same way as the mathematics expert explained and modeled instruction for them. At the end of the lesson study session, the facilitator said, "Now, I understand who the knowledgeable other in the lesson study research team should be. A mathematics teacher in a school may not have deep enough knowledge; perhaps we need true experts to be in this role?" The university partnership has continued with reciprocal benefit.

A second example can be seen at Deerwood Elementary School. In 1984, Deerwood Elementary School opened to serve a growing suburban area, but over time the community changed to one with 53 percent students receiving free or reduced lunch benefits. As the school community changed, student achievement began a downward trend as teachers, who had experienced success, were hesitant to alter their previously successful instructional practices.

Principal McHale was appointed to the position and sought support from the university, resulting in a partnership in which university teacher candidates were in the school for their required service learning, field experiences, and formal internships. University teacher candidates provided over 2,540 hours of teaching one to one or in small groups during one school year! Additionally, the university faculty partners provided professional learning for the teachers, particularly on using digital tools to engage students' thinking and improve reading. This partnership was aptly named, Boots on the Ground, in which teacher candidates began teaching high-needs elementary children and learning how to successfully meet students' learning needs.

Learning results are impressive. The students outperformed 120 other school district elementary schools and were ranked second in the school district in science in 2014. The increase in science scores relates to the assistance with reading and reading informational and nonfiction texts. Deerwood Elementary School won the Golden Apple Award for volunteer hours, and Principal McHale was honored with the Little Red School House Award from the Florida Association of School Administrators (FASA) in 2015.

Capacity was developed among the teachers as they learned from the teacher candidates and the university faculty partners. An added capacity building perk is that the principal identified the teacher candidates who he believed were the best fit for his school and targeted them for paid tutoring. Then, he offered them teaching contracts upon graduation. Collaborative partnerships provide reciprocal benefit. To learn more about this partnership to develop capacity, go to http://www.authorstream.com/Presentation/Deerwood1601-2477176-deerwood-elementary-little-red-schoolhouse/.

FEEDBACK

Once the expectations are clear and the learner's goal for coaching has been self-determined, then feedback should be specific, timely, and relate to the self-determined goal. Feedback has an effect size of $d = 0.75$ when it meets the criteria of being specific, relevant, and timely (Hattie, 2009, 2012). However, if feedback is not aligned with these criteria, the probability of improvement would not have such a high probability.

Relevancy may not seem like a necessary element in feedback that generates improvement, but sometimes feedback can be irrelevant to the learner's goal. For example, if the learner's goal is to ask more moderate- to high-level questions and the coaching feedback is that students were tapping their pencils or distracting others, is the feedback relevant? Student behaviors that are distracting others may be something for the learner to consider, but most likely uninvited feedback will be viewed as criticism, when it is not directly related to the self-directed learning goal. If criticism is perceived, rather than feedback related to the self-directed learning goal, then it is unlikely that the learner will request coaching in the future.

Coaching is not reflection alone but should include purposeful actionable authentic feedback to improve student learning. Coaches' and mentors' feedback can nourish growth through candor (Sherman & Frea, 2004). Authentic feedback indicates that the coach is invested in the learner's success enough to be clear and specific in providing the feedback.

Reflect upon these two examples of coaching feedback after a walkthrough in which the teacher invited students to generate their lived experiences in applying the scientific method. The teacher's learning goal was to improve engagement and accuracy application of the scientific method.

1. You are an amazing teacher! No wonder all of the parents request you to be their children's teacher. The students seemed to be engaged. How did you feel about the lesson?
2. I noticed that fifteen of the twenty-two students were writing examples of the steps they had completed of the scientific method. The other seven seemed to be less confident in what they needed to generate. I wonder how their examples may have been different if you had modeled first (direct instruction), followed by pairs generating the examples (guided practice)?

Consider a popular feedback model that includes giving two positive statements to build rapport and one negative statement of something to work on. In the authors' observation of implementation of this model, most of the coaching time is spent focusing on general feedback that feels good (two positive statements), and any improvement target is slipped in quickly, if at all, at the end of the discussion. While feeling good is important, it is not enough to improve effectiveness. Professionals develop confidence and self-efficacy when they are effective and have positive and measurable results.

Productive coaching, mentoring, and leading are grounded in effective adult communication that is authentic and targets the learner's self-identified goal. When time is short and the learner has identified the target goal, it may be that the entire feedback is positive or that only one generative statement or reflective query about getting closer to the learning goal is appropriate. Notice that there is no negative statement suggested. By focusing on the learner's self-directed goal, the entire allocated time for coaching can focus on feedback, reflection, modeling, practicing, and next steps for continual development of expertise.

COLLABORATION

Schools and school districts with collaborative cultures outperform those that are not collaborative (Hargreaves & Fullan, 2012). True collaboration is voluntary, participants are equal during the interactions, and they share a mutual goal (Friend, et al., 2010). In collaborative school or school district cultures, the collective wisdom is sought and collectively the stakeholders own the responsibility for student learning outcomes.

Instructional Planning

There are many forms of collaboration and one of the most common is collaborative instructional planning with time provided. Teachers who teach the same standards meet together to discuss the best order of instruction. Order of instruction includes systematic scaffolding from introduction and direct instruction to guided practice, to independent practice, and mastery, followed by assessment (Taylor, et al., 2014). Coach Melissa shared that she had a misconception about assessment. She thought it was independent practice. When she began coaching teachers to have independent practice prior to assessment, the teachers' student learning outcomes improved.

While their learners will differ, the standards taught will not differ. Therefore, instructional differentiation plays a role in teacher effectiveness. Elements that can be adjusted for individuals or groups are instructional strategies, time for learning, student to teacher ratio (individual, group, or class), and resources.

Instructional differentiation for those who have demonstrated mastery is as important as for those who have not demonstrated mastery. Differentiation upward means providing learning tasks for students to think more deeply. Or, learning tasks can be more complex or include more reading and analysis of complex texts. One of the most effective methods of differentiation upward is to raise the level of thinking needed to be successful with the learning task: analysis, synthesis, evaluation, or creating new knowledge. Please note that differentiation upward is not more learning tasks, nor is it tutoring another student. The advanced learner deserves the same expectation of differentiation as the one who has not yet developed mastery of the target standard.

Data and Evidence Study

Data and evidence study is another collaborative process in which the coaches, mentors, administrators, and learners collect and review data and evidence of student learning. Data and evidence are used to ascertain what is being learned, by whom, and under what conditions. Note that the elements of evidence to consider include the components of the standard or leading to the standard that have been learned by students and the strategies that worked or did not work well for them.

Data and evidence study supports instructional differentiation among students within one class or across two or more teachers' classes. Intervention and acceleration of learning follows data and evidence study through instructional differentiation.

Through data and evidence study, the question of alignment with standards of student learning tasks, order of instruction, scaffolding, instructional strategies, and assessments may arise. Sometimes these elements are not aligned as the rigor of the instruction may be less than that of the standards or of items on assessments.

As noted in chapter 5, expertise with the academic language of rigor (e.g., top or bottom number or numerator or denominator) is important to assure that instructional language and student learning tasks are aligned with the rigor of targeted standards and assessments. To realize improvements in student learning on accountability measures, alignment of rigor and academic language need to be present. Purposeful and deliberate instruction, modeling, and practicing aligned academic language with students improve outcomes.

Instructional Rounds or Walkthroughs

Instructional rounds or walkthroughs as collaborative visits with follow-up discussions can be helpful for achieving a common understanding and creating a mental model of effective instruction (Elmore, et al., 2009). When the teacher's learning intentions are clear to students and supported by evidence-based instruction, the walkthrough team will easily identify these elements.

Coach, mentor, administrator, and learner may compose the walkthrough team and note the target professional behaviors and how well the implementation is proceeding. Through the collaborative walkthroughs, the team will acquire more expertise and their conclusions will be more calibrated as they see instruction through each other's eyes.

In the follow-up discussion, the team or those in the coaching partnership will identify the on-target professional practices, engage in coaching, and identify next steps. Everyone will develop clearer mental models of effective instruction.

Similarly, in a diverse school district, the authors collaborated with a superintendent to improve literacy learning across four high schools with systematic professional learning, walkthroughs, and coaching of literacy teachers, assistant principals, and literacy coaches. Walkthroughs in each other's classes focused on self-identified professional practices for which participants gave feedback in the form of (1) I like the way you . . . and (2) I wonder if. . .

Over the two-year period of the collaboration, each high school increased reading proficiency by a mean of 4 percent and the range of students making one year's growth rose from 15 percent to 28 percent (Taylor & Gordon, 2014). The coaching partnership process was critical to teachers' success.

Administrators are busy and have competing priorities. Sometimes they may visit classes without follow-up discussions or the provision of feedback and coaching. Principals who use walkthroughs as professional learning and provide specific feedback see more improvement in student learning in their schools than those who do not do so (Grisson, et al., 2013).

For more examples of how to provide feedback as instructional leaders, coaches, and mentors, you may want to review *The Instructional Leader and the Brain: Using Neuroscience to Inform Practice* (Glick, 2011). To create a culture of active caring, consider authentic feedback as a demonstration of commitment to the success of one another (Taylor, 2010). The coaching partnership members should be committed to providing helpful feedback after each class visit to improve learning and to demonstrate respect for the learner.

SCENARIO: STEM TEACHERS LEARNING WITH MIXED REALITY EXPERIENCES

Novice STEM teachers were excited to practice introducing a standards-based lesson that they had co-developed. They were particularly looking forward to this experience because the class would be made up of TLE TeachLivE™ middle school avatars. (Mixed reality is a method that incorporates both digital technology and people to provide avatar interactions in real-time, specific to the participant.) The teachers had been introduced to the mixed reality method before preparing the lesson introduction and knew that the avatar middle school students each had a different personality, would act similar to students in any middle school classroom, and would even have digital devices.

Pairs of STEM teachers arrived at the appointed time with a colleague to introduce the selected lesson. One teacher introduced a lesson for 10 minutes while the colleague and coach observed, and then provided feedback. Next, the second teacher introduced the lesson, followed by feedback from the first teacher and the coach.

The teachers were surprised that if they started to lecture or drone on, one avatar student put her head down, another started texting, and a third tried to redirect the teacher to something more interesting by making comments and asking questions! On the other hand, when Alex used engagement strategies, the avatar middle school students seemed to respond positively by raising a hand to comment, by nodding as if understanding, or by picking up a pencil to write.

After the mixed reality experience, each teacher was asked to provide coaching related to how this particular experience was helpful in improving lesson introductions. The teachers were unanimous that they liked the practice with the avatars and the feedback, and wanted an opportunity to try again. In the teachers' written reflections, they indicated that the most helpful portion of the mixed reality experience was the feedback from the coach (Speir, 2015). While they liked getting the perspective of their peer teachers, they thought the peer teacher benefitted from observing and listening to the feedback given to another by the knowledgeable coach.

Inquiry-driven learning and expertise development is grounded in queries or wonders that come to your mind. After generating wonders, self-directed learners seek to find answers or a deeper understanding. What do you wonder after reading this scenario?

- How can the avatars respond in real time?
- What would happen if the teachers practiced with the avatars without feedback from a coach?
- Would the feedback from a peer be as helpful as that from a coach?

Use what you know about adult learning, coaching, and giving feedback or seek another's thinking (virtually or in person) to answer your own questions. To learn more about TeachLivE™ mixed reality, you may want to go to www.youtube.com/watch?v=DWrTRSmIGuM.

TIPS FOR CONTINUAL DEVELOPMENT OF EXPERTISE

For continuous learning in the coaching partnership to build the capacity of the school and school district, reciprocal accountability will be present (Fink

& Markholt, 2011). Everyone in the partnership is accountable for each other's continuous improvement.

Learner

Learners are responsible for their own continuous improvement. However, it is up to you to ask for support and to present the disposition of openness to others. Although the focus is on giving authentic feedback to others with candor to nurture their improvement, when you invite feedback, there is an even greater probability that you will enhance your expertise (Hattie, 2009). Supporting this important finding is a study of eighty-one STEM teachers and their mentors. The STEM teachers voiced that they became more effective as first year teachers as a result of the feedback, relationship, and coaching from their mentors (Karcinski, 2015).

Use your digital devices to maximize opportunities for self-reflection and collaboration with others. An application from Google Play that may be useful is Sibme App. With this application you can record yourself, and as you review the video, you can annotate in regard to your self-identified goal. You can share with your mentor, coach, or administrator any part that you like or not at all like. Collaborative review may enhance opportunities for coaching and improvement even if the coaches, mentors, or administrators are not available when you are practicing the target professional behavior.

Coach and Mentor

An effective practice is to collaborate and co-plan instruction (Hattie, 2012). Whether the co-planning takes place with all who teach the same standards or only the coach or mentor with the learner, it is a practice that leverages the knowledge and skill of all who collaborate.

Invite feedback from the learners and you will find that you learn the most when the learners provide you feedback (Hattie, 2012). Mentors consistently indicate that they learn from other mentors, coaches, and from their mentees as well (Karcinski, 2015). Also, these mentors shared that they had to think back in time to when they were novice teachers and when their teaching practices were not automatic or fluent (Karcinski, 2015). Through this reflection and breaking down the effective practices into little steps, they were able to share in small chunks of practices to incrementally support development of improved expertise of their mentees.

As coaches and mentors, you are encouraged to continually investigate accessible research-based resources. Be active in your local, state, and national professional organizations and regularly read journals provided by these organizations. The articles within will be vetted by knowledgeable editors.

Check out the nonprofit resources, such as digitalpromise.org and the interactive researchmap.digitalpromise.org to review learning sciences articles, summaries, or to discover research-based professional practices. Another nonprofit resource that is focused on project-based learning, particularly for Advanced Placement courses, is Lucas Education Research (lerportal. org). Investigate other reliable sources, such as Research for Better Teaching (RBTeach.com).

Administrator

As administrators you are encouraged to seek coaching in the context of your responsibility (Salavert, 2015). To transform student learning, you are to model learning about rigorous instruction, standards-based instructional planning, and alignment of standards with instructional plans and with assessment.

You need a mental model of effective practice to easily recognize it, as well as for recognizing ineffective practice. You are responsible for modeling and being explicit about expected professional practices to improve the learning and coaching culture (Elmore, 2004). Such modeling may begin with sharing your values and beliefs that led to your professional practices.

REFLECTIVE PRACTICE TO CONTINUALLY IMPROVE EXPERTISE

Learner

When you review the Coaching System Planning Tool in Appendix A, put a star beside the areas of expertise in which you believe you are an expert. Place a question mark beside each of the areas of expertise that you believe you would like to set as self-directed learning goals.

Write down your preferred five instructional strategies that you use most frequently. After writing them down, look in one of the Hattie texts or go to http://visible-learning.org/ and find the effect size for your preferred instructional strategies. Are there alternate strategies you may implement in place of your top five or do these strategies have high enough effect sizes for your students' learning? When you implement strategies, do you do so with fidelity?

Ask your students to provide you feedback. When you learn the easiest, what do I do as a teacher? In this class, when is learning the most difficult?

Coach and Mentor

When you review the Coaching System Planning Tool in Appendix A, put a star beside the areas of expertise in which you believe you are an expert.

Place a question mark beside each area of expertise that you believe you would like to set as a self-directed learning goal.

Write down your preferred five instructional strategies that you use most frequently when modeling for others or in professional learning. After writing them down, look in one of the Hattie texts or go to http://visible-learning.org/ and find the effect size for your preferred instructional strategies. Are there alternate strategies you may implement in place of your top five, or do these strategies have high-effect sizes for your context?

Ask those you coach and mentor to provide you with feedback. What do I do that supports your learning? What can I do to be a more effective mentor and/or coach?

Administrator

When you review the Coaching System Planning Tool in Appendix A, put a star beside the areas of expertise in which you believe you are an expert. Place a question mark beside each of the areas of expertise that you believe you would like to set as a self-directed learning goal.

Write down the five instructional strategies that you see the most effective teachers using and the five that you see less effective teachers using. Note the five strategies you see teachers of rigorous courses using and teachers of high-needs students using. Do the strategies differ among these sets of teachers or are they the same? If the strategies are similar, are they implemented similarly and with fidelity?

After writing down the strategies in the groups, compare the effect sizes of the strategies used by the groups. You may want to look in one of the Hattie texts or go to http://visible-learning.org/ and find the effect size for these instructional strategies. Are there alternate strategies you may use when coaching others or do the strategies most observed have high-effect sizes that will result in broad improvement of learning?

Model Reciprocal Accountability and practice inquiry to improve your leadership practice. Ask your fellow administrators, coaches, mentors, and teachers to share examples of when you have helped them to think more deeply. Think about when you have assisted them in being more purposeful and deliberate, resulting in improved student learning.

- What did I do when I helped you to have better learning outcomes?
- Please share with me an action you would like me to take to support your continued development of expertise.
- What evidence can you share with me that I have developed a culture of collaboration and active caring in our school/school district?

DEFINITIONS

Feedback	Authentic nonjudgmental comments related to the self-identified learning goal.
Fluency	Appropriate rate and accuracy.
Reciprocal accountability	Each person in the partnership is accountable to the other for learning and continuous improvement.
Self-efficacy	Believing that one's actions will have intended results.

RESOURCES

Center for Educational Leadership. (www.K–12leadership.org).

Fink, S. & Markholt, A. (2011). *Leading for Instructional Improvement: How Successful Leaders Develop Teaching and Learning Expertise.* San Francisco: Jossey-Bass.

Glick, M. (2011). *The Instructional Leader and the Brain: Using Neuroscience to Inform Practice.* Thousand Oaks, CA: Corwin Press.

Hargraves, A. & Fullan, M. (2012). *Professional Capital: Transforming Teaching in Every School.* New York: Teachers College Press.

Hattie, J. (2012). *Visible Learning for Teachers: Maximizing Impact on Learning.* New York: Routledge.

Hattie, J. (2009). *Visible Learning: A Synthesis of 800+ Meta-Analyses on Achievement.* New York: Routledge.

INVEST Video Library Model Lessons.

Lewis, C. C. & Hurd, J. (2011). *Lesson Study Step by Step: How Teacher Learning Communities Improve Instruction.* Portsmouth, NH: Heinemann.

Lucas Education Research (lerportal.org).

Research for Better Teaching (www.RBTeach.com).

Researchmap.digitalpromise.org.

Saphier, J., Halye-Speca, M. A., & Gower, R. (2008). *The Skillful Teacher: Building Your Teaching Skills.* Acton, MA: Research for Better Teaching, Inc.

Sibme App (Google Play).

Taylor, R. T., Watson, R., & Nutta, J. (2014). *Leading, Teaching, Learning Common Core Standards: Rigorous Expectations for All Students.* Lanham, MD: Rowman Education.

Taylor, R. T. (2010). *Leading Learning: Change Student Achievement Today!* Thousand Oaks, CA: Corwin Press.

Taylor, R. T. (2007). *Improving Reading, Writing, and Content Learning.* Thousand Oaks, CA: Corwin Press.

Chapter 8

Commitment to Empowerment

Followed by the principal, the teacher is the most important influence in student learning (Wenglisky, 2000; Sanders & Rivers, 1996). Principals are responsible for whole-school improvement and change in student learning outcomes (Ippolito, 2010). On the other hand, coaches and mentors have responsibility for an individual's improvement in effectiveness, which impacts whole-school improvement (Ippolito, 2010). This kind of thinking is why the partnership is important as a way to think about coaching and mentoring.

As you have read and discussed the concepts and tips advocated for within this text with valued colleagues, no doubt you have considered expertise necessary for productive coaching partnerships: clearly communicated roles, generative thinking, strategic relationship development, and effective adult communication. These areas of expertise are essential for successful implementation of the coaching partnership process that was shared in chapter 6. Without the development of essential expertise you might hypothesize that coaching and mentoring may be ineffective, not resulting in improvement in effectiveness or student learning outcomes. Through exploration of essential skills and continual development of professional expertise, the foundation has been laid for this last chapter.

Commitment to effective coaching and mentoring systems is demonstrated in a number of ways. Personal and professional resource allocation reflects the level of commitment to systematic processes by learners, coaches, mentors, and administrators for effective partnerships to improve student learning. Commitment is reflected in time, personnel, and funds, along with empowerment of others through their continuous development of expertise (chapter 7).

Improvement and development of coaching partnerships is not an event but a process overtime with feedback and enhancements (chapter 6). To prevent overlearning to automaticity of ineffective strategies through practice, the coaches' and mentors' facilitation of reflective practice and feedback is within the coaching partnership process (chapter 6).

These partnerships are intended to improve effectiveness of all those involved in the partnership, particularly the effectiveness of teachers who have the most critical role related to student learning. Enhancing expertise in the complexity of teaching requires "time, practice, and experience" (Ambrosetti, 2010, p. 117).

Commitment also includes monitoring successive improvements in professional practice, reflection, and generation of next steps for the coach and mentor, learner, and administrator. Successful partnerships to improve student learning are characterized by "an in-depth relationship involving critical feedback and mutual support" (Washburn-Moses, 2010, p. 4) and not just a few meetings with a designated colleague.

For school-wide change to occur, it takes commitment beyond the coaching partnership. However, when the coaching culture is developed around collaboration for continuous improvement in effectiveness and assurance of equitable learning outcomes for all learners, large-scale improvements are possible. Motivation naturally emerges from individuals believing that their contributions and inputs are valued. They have self-efficacy and believe that their work is important and yields impact resulting in improved student learning. Evidence of their impact and belief in the value of the work is motivational (Amabile & Kramer, 2011).

SCENARIO: EMPOWERMENT THROUGH THE COACHING PARTNERSHIP

In an urban, diverse high school of 2800 students, the new principal, Dr. Bradshaw, developed a coaching team with one coach for each content area: literacy, English language arts, mathematics, science, social studies, and electives. Annually, the school saw increased student enrollment which, when combined with natural faculty attrition, necessitated the hiring of new teachers.

Often, these new teachers had no formal preparation for teaching, resulting in the need for a coach dedicated to the success of those newly hired. As a digital school, there was a need for a digital coach to support teacher and student engagement with digital tools to accelerate student learning. These factors resulted in a coaching team of eight who worked closely with the school administrative team, department chairs, and mentors to form the leadership team.

The leadership team committed to the coaching partnership by protecting the coach's work time and providing the resource of time for learners to practice, receive feedback, reflect, and try again. Generally, the coach modeled for the teacher as learner, followed by co-teaching, followed by observing the learner with feedback. Those in the partnership reflected and shared commitment to their improved professional practice. Last, the administrators, coaches, and mentors reflected upon what they learned during these experiences and noted their next steps.

Annually, the coaching team, administrators, and university partner met to review the school's Literacy System, celebrate achievements, consider improvements, and update the system with new evidence-based goals (Taylor & Gunter, 2006). The Literacy System served as the guide for improvement in effectiveness by all those in the coaching partnership.

This process had been used for the previous three years to assure collaboration that considered everyone's voice, to agree upon actions, and to develop commitment to the system. The system recommended that revisions be shared with faculty, staff, and administrators and their input sought prior to finalization and implementation in the next school year.

During this fourth annual collaboration, the group of coaches identified the strengths of collaboration between the literacy and English language arts coach and the evidence of changes in the after-school student tutoring design. The team of coaches created a rotational tutoring plan so that the students would not get bored with long expanses of time focused on one concept or skill. They also added a no-cost incentive for students who were consistent in tutoring participation; students received an athletic pass for the entire next school year! Positive response to the athletic pass incentive was huge and valued by the other students who cheered when passes were delivered to tutored students during the school day.

Readers may wonder if the change and incentives were symbolic or did the redesign of the tutoring and increased participation have any measureable results? Yes, the reading and English language arts results saw a 10 percent improvement over the previous school year.

Other identified strengths in the previous year's Literacy System included the clarity of roles and the content-specific goals. It was mentioned that English learners seemed particularly responsive to the student-friendly writing rubric, collaboratively designed the year before and implemented across content areas.

Concerns were raised to be considered in revisions for the Literacy System. The need for implementation fidelity by all faculty was noted. Participants also requested that goals be set to assist with a consistently used common academic language, reading, writing, and mathematical word problems. The team of coaches also suggested that instructional strategies specific to content classes be more highly supported by coaches and mentors. The last new goal identified was to increase rigor in student learning tasks.

As the annual collaborative session came to a close, the university partner reflected on the high level of engagement, expertise in research-based instruction, adult communication and collaboration, and reflective practice among members of this coaching team. They were self-regulated and self-led, and even set the identified stretch goals for themselves. Each committed to collaboration and effort to assure that the students had equity in learning outcomes, *not just equitable opportunities to learn.*

Dr. Bradshaw had empowered the team to determine their work for the next school year, while assuring them of the resources to accomplish goals that they believed would be best. The Literacy System was the vehicle that she used to guide the school, to develop expertise, and to empower the faculty.

Sam, one of these expert coaches, shared that during his twenty-eight-year career, the experience of being an instructional coach in this high school with this principal was the first time that he had truly been empowered. Sam now believed in himself as the principal had developed his self-efficacy and added, "I wouldn't go anywhere else. I've never been told before that I had the answers and that the principal had such confidence in me."

Through the coaching partnership and the development of empowered experts, Dr. Bradshaw had created a problem for herself. The mentors, coaches, teachers, and administrators had been given the gifts of expertise and empowerment. They were considered more highly skilled than those in similar positions in other schools.

As a result, these professionals were in high demand to provide consultation to other schools and school districts, to lead professional learning in other schools and the school district. Due to their data and evidence-supported effectiveness, they were regularly offered promotions and higher compensation by other principals and school district administrators. The principal who is an instructional leader develops others and has a never-ending task of continuing to discover and prepare teachers, coaches, mentors, and other administrators. There is no better evidence of leadership.

LEADERS AND SUSTAINABLE CHANGE

For sustainable and long-term change, the school or school district culture should focus on eliminating ineffective professional or instructional practices to be replaced with more effective ones. A coaching culture should not represent more work or commitment from those in the coaching partnership.

Mark Shanoff, principal of Ocoee Middle School, found that persistence in modeling expectations and professional learning, coupled with a strong coaching partnership of teachers, coaches, and administrators, reduced the achievement gap between student groups (Taylor & Shanoff, 2015). From 2012 through 2014, the percent of students scoring proficient on the Florida Comprehensive Achievement Test (FCAT) Reading rose from 56 percent to 64 percent, FCAT Mathematics rose from 59 percent to 62 percent, FCAT Writing rose from 37 percent to 48 percent, and FCAT Science rose from 44 percent to 54 percent. A feat difficult to achieve was the reduction in the gap between white and black students from 22.7 percent to 7.6 percent and the gap between white and Hispanic students from 22 percent to 14 percent (Taylor & Shanoff, 2015).

Like Mark and the coaches, mentors, and teachers at OMS, all are to be consistent in modeling the cultural beliefs, values, and practices expected of others. If collaboration in instructional planning is expected, then administrators, coaches, and mentors will participate in co-planning. Likewise, if cognitive engagement is a value, then administrators will put their digital devices out of sight, as will others, when collaborating.

To accomplish large-scale change and empowerment, leaders have to continuously improve their own leadership practice and the leadership practice of others. The Center for Educational Leadership at the University of Washington has developed resources that may support your continuous improvement (www.K–12leadership.org).

TIPS FOR A PRODUCTIVE COACHING PARTNERSHIP

Many of the tips in this chapter represent those collaboratively generated by coaches, mentors, teachers, and administrators when asked to think about what each should know and do. These tips are practical, aligned with the preceding chapters, and the research on developing a coaching culture focused on learning through collaborations that are built on individual's strengths (Taylor, 2010).

Learner

Learners may not have control over time nor over financial resources, but they control their disposition relative to the coaching partnership. Commitment to the partnership lies in commitment to students' learning outcomes and to generative thinking. Teachers indicated that you know your strengths and weakness and need to share them with your coach and mentor. Also, bring your relationship with the K–12 students to the partnership, along with the data and evidence of their learning successes and learning challenges.

These professionals also indicated that you are responsible to share the expectations of your administrator, as expectations given to you may not be explicitly known by a coach or mentor. Finally, you are to bring your time and undivided attention to the coaching and mentoring partnership while trusting the coach or mentor-learner relationship.

Coach and Mentor

Commitment to the learner and to the improvement of each student's learning as a measure of effectiveness is essential. Coaches and mentors who align their work time with the coaching purpose and measured outcomes are most successful.

Coaches and mentors bring to the partnership the school's goals, strengths, and weaknesses. You should know the administrators' expectations, how they communicate, and how they hold others accountable for expectations. Understanding the standards upon which instructional plans are to be developed and owning research-based, high-effect size instructional strategies are essential to support teachers' improvement in effectiveness. You also need access to resources to share.

Consider the best professional learning to be job-embedded that can be implemented immediately. Workshops followed by coaching are more effective than workshops without follow-up coaching. This coaching may take various forms: assistance with instructional planning, modeling or co-teaching lessons, observing lessons, and providing coaching feedback while inviting feedback for themselves. To successfully accomplish these suggestions, as coaches and mentors you have to own the coaching partnership process.

A few additional tips are offered for mentors, since you may have fewer learners than the coach. In most instances, mentors provide content- or subject-specific support. Therefore, access to content-specific resources, labs, and supplemental materials is needed. Understand the school district policies, school policies, and guidelines on which the learners must be compliant and help reduce extraneous or conflicting information, particularly for new teachers. Knowing and sharing contact information for "go to people" within the school and school district can reduce frustration on the part of the learners.

Learners' energies can be focused on effective instruction and not on other important but noninstructional aspects of being an educator. Finally, mentors have the additional responsibility of being advocates for learners with the understanding that professional behavior change takes time, even with learners who have a positive outlook toward improvement and who exert their best personal efforts.

Administrator

Consider how you frame coaching and mentoring in your school, school district, or organization. You are encouraged to frame and communicate coaching and mentoring as a collaborative process that contributes to everyone's improvement in effectiveness to result in improved learning outcomes.

Reflect on your commitment to the coaching partnership and the extent to which school and school district resources are aligned to (1) prepare coaches to be effective leaders and mentors, (2) provide the time for coaches to coach and learners to be coached, (3) provide learning resources, and (4) participation by leaders in the partnership processes (Taylor, et al., 2013). This commitment will provide a return on investment (ROI) that will most likely not be realized unless coaching time is protected and expertise strategically developed, resulting in capacity development of the entire organization.

One of the most important tips shared by groups of mentors, coaches, and administrators is that it is the administrator's responsibility to collaboratively develop clear roles and to communicate those roles to all stakeholders. In addition, roles should be aligned with how you frame and fund the coaching partnership. A way to clarify expectations is to provide non-negotiables of evidence-based instructional practices, supported by clear priorities for focus and use of time by all in the coaching and mentoring partnership (Taylor, 2010).

A basic concept of instructional leadership is that you cannot lead without expertise in the area to be led. Most likely, administrators develop their content expertise and knowledge of the standards by participating with coaches, mentors, and teachers in professional learning and collaborative instructional planning. Total delegation without enough expertise to know the level of expertise of the coaches and mentors will not yield positive outcomes.

The word "data" has become negative in many schools and school districts. There is so much data that finding meaningful data and knowing how to use data to improve student learning has become a challenge. Administrators have the responsibility of providing meaningful data that are usable and can easily be applied in instructional decision-making at the teacher level. You also should engage in partnership discussions of how to determine data and evidence that are credible, questions that data raise, and steps for using data to differentiate instruction for students and coaching for learners.

Throughout the authors' sessions with teachers, mentors, coaches, and administrators, there were seemingly soft, but important tips shared. Teachers, mentors, and coaches suggested that administrators are to be open-minded and flexible in their thinking. Be a bridge between coaches and teachers. Most importantly, they emphasized that administrators are to build a coaching culture focused not only on students' learning but also on the learning of adults. That is, the school is to be a safe place for all learners, including teachers.

Motivate positively by developing others and providing autonomy through empowerment (Pink, 2011). Remember to celebrate small steps in progress toward the target goals and demonstrate value for everyone (Amabile & Kramer, 2011).

REFLECTIVE PRACTICE

In each chapter, reflective practice has been encouraged. At this time, reflect on the authentic scenario in this chapter. Although your context may be smaller and may not include as many coaches and mentors, think about how you can work collaboratively to build one another's expertise, leading to empowerment in your professional practice.

- When your coaching and mentoring team collaborates, is everyone's voice listened to and respected?
- Do you collaboratively develop the direction or system for the next school year?
- Has expertise been developed so that expectations are self-generated at a higher level annually?
- Are coaches, mentors, and administrators prepared to be empowered to make decisions and recommend actions to improve student learning?
- Have the administrators developed self-efficacy of those in the coaching and mentoring partnership?
- What commitments do you make to improve the coaching and mentoring partnership?

Review Appendix A, Coaching Partnership System Planning Tool: Coach, Mentor, Learner, and Administrator Potential Actions and Next Steps. Collaborate with those in your coaching and mentoring partnership to complete the right column of next steps. Annually, collaboratively revisit the partnership and consider how each will gain more expertise and contribute during the next school year. Finally, celebrate the successes along the way and be sure to provide positive and encouraging words to all those in the partnership.

FINAL THOUGHTS

Everyone in the coaching partnership is a leader. Leaders develop others and themselves. They do not forge ahead alone. An investment of a few minutes in coaching saves time and effort later as less intervention will be needed.

Your legacy is the development and empowerment of others to achieve their goals. Through others' actions and communications to improve student learning, your influence will be exponential.

RESOURCES

Amabile, T. & Kramer, S. (2011). *The Progress Principle.* Boston: Harvard Business Review Press.

Pink, D. H. (2011). *Drive: The Surprising Truth About What Motivates* Us. New York: Riverhead Books.

Taylor, R. T. & Gunter, G. (2006). *The Literacy Leadership Fieldbook.* Thousand Oaks, CA: Corwin Press.

Taylor, R. T. (2010). *Leading Learning: Change Student Achievement Today!* Thousand Oaks, CA: Corwin Press.

Appendix A

Coaching System Planning Tool

Coaching System Planning Tool: Coach, Mentor, Learner, and Administrator Potential Actions and Next Steps

Expertise	Coach and Mentor Action	Learner Action	Administrator Action	Your Next Steps
Content Chapter 1	Recognize gaps between learner knowledge and the level required for standards-based instruction. Ask questions to prompt self-reflection. Share resources.	Understand the target standards' content deeply enough to ensure that students achieve expected outcomes. Ask mentor and coach for assistance.	Recognize gaps in content knowledge. Employ deep content knowledge. Ask, "What are the content learning needs of teachers, coaches, and administrators?"	
Curriculum Chapter 1	Know standards-based curriculum components. Help teachers identify curriculum gaps.	Know and implement the standards-based curriculum. Ask mentor and coach for assistance.	Assure standards-aligned curriculum. Ask, "What do we need to do to assure implementation?"	
Research-based Pedagogy Chapters 1–8	Know the non-negotiable evidence-based instructional practices. Model evidence-based practices and use of resources. Invite learner to observe you and provide reflection.	Engage students with evidence-based instructional practices. Model and represent target standards to result in students' new understanding. Ask mentor and coach for feedback.	Determine non-negotiable evidence-based practices. Provide accountability for evidence-based practice. Ask, "What support is needed for consistent research-based instruction?"	
Student Engagement Chapter 1	Notice student engagement. Identify student opportunities for inquiry, asking questions, and thinking with rigor. Share role model examples.	Encourage student thinking at application, synthesis, and analysis levels. Plan for cognitive presence throughout the lesson.	Listen to students during learning and review their work. Celebrate role models. Ask, "How will you engage all and know who is engaged?"	

(Continued)

Coaching System Planning Tool: Coach, Mentor, Learner, and Administrator Potential Actions and Next Steps *(Continued)*

Expertise	Coach and Mentor Action	Learner Action	Administrator Action	Your Next Steps
Learning Environment Chapter 1	Share effective classroom organization and management. Ask questions to help learner self-identify focus areas. Help learners define, model, and practice classroom routines.	Structure for smooth routines. Ask coach and mentor to model. Increase engaged time with smooth/rapid transitions. Provide clear expectations. Foster self-monitoring.	Create a common vision for safe, respectful learning environments. Develop model classrooms. Ask, "What do you need to assure an environment that maximizes learning?"	
Roles Chapter 2	Clarify your role with the administrator. Identify his or her professional learning goals. Ask, "What is the priority for use of my time?"	Know the expectations of support given to your mentor and coach. Know the expectations of the administrator for you in the coaching partnership Ask, "I wonder how much time I should expect to be with my coach and mentor?"	Be clear about the roles of each in the coaching partnership. Clarify the differences in the roles of mentors and coaches. Clarify your expectations of the learner. Ask, "What can I do to assure a successful coaching partnership?"	
Generative Thinking Chapter 3	Model generative thinking. Model belief that effort yields results. Model thinking at levels of application, analysis, and evaluation. Act on the belief that ability can be developed.	Embrace generative thinking for yourself and students. Model generative thinking and belief in the development of intelligence. Provide every student the same opportunity to achieve. Differentiate support.	Establish a generative-thinking school culture. Model that effort yields results. Model belief that intelligence and achievement can be developed. Model what if thinking. Ask, "What actions result in students exceeding expectations?"	
Relationships Chapter 4	Deliberately cultivate relationships. Support learners with reflection. Build trust and rapport. Invite feedback.	Value the partnership relationship and feedback. Model the value of relationships in interactions with students. Be predictable with students.	Build trust. Cultivate student, teacher, coach, and mentor relationships. Ask, "How can I support your coach/mentor/learner relationships?"	

(Continued)

Coaching System Planning Tool: Coach, Mentor, Learner, and Administrator Potential Actions and Next Steps *(Continued)*

Expertise	Coach and Mentor Action	Learner Action	Administrator Action	Your Next Steps
Academic Language Chapter 5	Model academic language. Know the research for developing academic language. Provide practice opportunities for learners with feedback.	Teach, model, and practice general and specific academic language. Apply academic language to new contexts.	Model and expect teaching, modeling, and practicing of academic language and research-based language acquisition. Ask, "How can we increase academic language modeling?"	
Communication Chapter 5	Model purposeful and deliberate communication using academic language. Value and respect the learner's point of view. Embrace different perspectives as collaboration opportunities.	Engage in honest conversations with mentor and coach related to trust, beliefs, values, and perspectives. Seek collaboration and consensus.	Establish a collaborative culture. Invite different perspectives. Value conversations and actively listen to student, teacher, coach. Ask, "How can I provide for your collaboration?"	
Data and Evidence Chapter 6	Identify evidences of student learning. Model data and evidence-informed instructional decision-making and adaptations. Use student work as artifacts for coaching and mentoring.	Explore evidences of students' learning or evidence that impacts students' learning. Monitor changes in data and evidence. Invite coach and mentor to provide perspectives.	Be explicit with how success looks, acts, and sounds. Celebrate evidence of success. Model data and evidence informed decision-making. Ask, "What evidence do you have that each student is learning?"	
Assessment Chapter 6	Ask questions to help teachers self-identify focus areas. Provide learners practice in identifying students thinking. Provide standards-aligned models of assessment. Highlight examples of success.	Structure lessons so that each student shares thinking. Use standards-aligned assessment. Provide feedback. Differentiate and adjust on the basis of evidence.	Assure standards-aligned assessment. Celebrate examples. View student and teacher evidence as a measure of administrator effectiveness. Ask, "How can I assist you to have greater learning?"	

Note: (1) Student means K–12 student (2) Learner may be teacher, mentor, coach, or administrator depending upon who is learning.

Additional Resources

Baines, L., & Fisher, J. (2013). *Teaching Challenging Texts: Fiction, Non-fiction, and Multi-media.* Lanham, MD: Rowman & Littlefield, Education Division.

Barkley, S. G. & Bianco, T. (2010). *Quality Teaching in a Culture of Coaching.* 2nd Edition. Lanham, MD: Rowman & Littlefield, Education Division.

Bonner, E. P. (2010). *Unearthing Culturally Responsive Mathematics Teaching.* Lanham, MD: Rowman & Littlefield, Education Division.

Costa, A. L. & Garmston, R. J. (2015). *Cognitive Caching: Developing Self-Directed Leaders and Learners.* Lanham, MD: Rowman & Littlefield, Education Division.

Ellison, J. L. & Hayes, C. (2013). *Cognitive Coaching: Weaving Threads of Learning and Change into the Culture of an Organization.* Lanham, MD: Rowman & Littlefield, Education Division.

Ellison, J. L. & Hayes, C. (2013). *Effective School Leadership: Developing Principals Through Cognitive Coaching.* Lanham, MD: Rowman & Littlefield, Education Division.

Fawcett, G. (2013). *Vocabulary in Action.* Lanham, MD: Rowman & Littlefield, Education Division.

Garmston, R. J., & Wellman, B. M. (2013). *The Adaptive School: A Sourcebook for Developing Collaborative Groups, 2nd edition.* Lanham, MD: Rowman & Littlefield, Education Division.

Glazer, S. M. (2013). *Words Matter: Teacher Language and Student Learning.* Lanham, MD: Rowman & Littlefield, Education Division.

Gray, G. & Donnelly, J. (2014). *History Repeats Itself in the Classroom, Tool: Prior Knowledge and Implementing the Common Core State Standards.* Lanham, MD: Rowman & Littlefield, Education Division.

Harris, A. S., Bruster, B., Peterson, B., & Shutt, T. (2010). *Examining and Facilitating Reflection to Improve Professional Practice.* Lanham, MD: Rowman & Littlefield, Education Division.

107

Manville, M. (2014). *Common Core State Standards for Grades K–1: Language Arts Instructional Strategies and Activities.* Lanham, MD: Rowman & Littlefield, Education Division.

Manville, M. (2014). *Common Core State Standards for Grades 2–3: Language Arts Instructional Strategies and Activities.* Lanham, MD: Rowman & Littlefield, Education Division.

Manville, M. (2014). *Common Core State Standards for Grades 4–5: Language Arts Instructional Strategies and Activities.* Lanham, MD: Rowman & Littlefield, Education Division.

Nelson-Reyes, A. M. (2013). *Success in School and Career: Common Core Standards in Language Arts K–5.* Lanham, MD: Rowman & Littlefield, Education Division.

Porton, H. D. (2014). *Closing the Gap between Risk and Resilience: How Struggling Learners can Cope with Common Core State Standards.* Lanham, MD: Rowman & Littlefield, Education Division.

Roseboro, A. J. S. (2013). *Teaching Reading in the Middle School: Common Core and More.* Lanham, MD: Rowman & Littlefield, Education Division.

Roseboro, A. J. S. (2013). *Teaching Writing in the Middle School: Common Core and More.* Lanham, MD: Rowman & Littlefield, Education Division.

Tomal, D. R. Schilling, C. A., & Wilhite, R. L. (2014). *Quality Teaching in a Culture of Coaching.* Lanham, MD: Rowman & Littlefield, Education Division.

References

Amabile, T. & Kramer, S. (2011). *The Progress Principle.* Boston: Harvard Business Review Press.

Ambrosetti, A. (2010). Mentors and Learning to Teach: What Do Pre-service Teachers Expect from their Mentor Teachers? *International Journal of Learning, 17*(9): 117–32.

Annenberg Institute for School Reform. (n.d.). *Instructional Coaching: Professional Development Strategies that Improve Instruction.* Retrieved May 2, 2015, from www.annenberginstitute.org/images/InstructionalCoaching.pdf.

Arneson, S. (2012). *Communicate and Motivate: The School Leader's Guide to Effective Communication.* Larchmont, NY: Eye on Education.

Bay-Williams, J. M. & Mc Gatha, M. (2014). *Mathematics Coaching: Resources and Tools for Coaches and Leaders, K–12.* Pearson.

Borman, J., Feger, S., & Kawakami, N. (2006). *Instructional Coaching: Key Themes from the Literature.* Providence, RI: The Education Alliance at Brown University.

Council of Chief State School Officers. (2013, April). Interstate Teacher Assessment and Support Consortium InTASC *Model Core Teaching Standards and Learning Progressions for Teachers 1.0: A Resource for Ongoing Teacher Development.* Washington, DC: Author.

Costa, A. L. & Garmston, R. J. (2015). *Cognitive Coaching: Developing Self-directed Leaders and Learners.* New York: Rowman & Littlefield.

Costa, A. L., & Garmston, R. J. (2002). *Cognitive Coaching: A Foundation for Renaissance Schools* (2nd ed.). Norwood, MA: Christopher-Gordon.

Costa, A. L. & Garmston, R. J. (1994). *Cognitive Coaching: A Foundation for Renaissance in Schools.* Norwood, MA: Christopher-Gordon.

Costa, A. & Kallick, B. (1993). Through the Lens of a Critical Friend. *Educational Leadership, 51*(2): 49–51.

Dole, J., & Donaldson, R. (2006). What Am I Supposed to Do All Day?: Three Big Ideas for the Reading Coach. *The Reading Teacher, 59*(5): 486–88.

Dweck, Carol S. (2006). *Mindset: The New Psychology of Success*. New York: Random House.

Edfuel.org. (2014). Map the Gap: *Confronting the Leadership Talent Gap in the New Urban Education Ecosystem*. Author.

Ellison, J. L. & Hayes, C. (2013). *Effective School Leadership: Developing Principals Through Cognitive Coaching*. Lanham, MD: Rowman & Littlefield, Education Division.

Ellison, J. L. & Hayes, C. (2006). *Cognitive Coaching: Weaving Threads of Learning and Change into the Culture of an Organization*. Norwood, MA: Christopher-Gordon.

Elmore, R. F. (2004). *School Reform from Inside Out: Policy, Practice, and Performance*. Cambridge, MA: Harvard Education Press.

Elmore, R. F., Furmen, S., & Teital, L. (2009). *Instructional Rounds in Education*. Cambridge, MA: Harvard Education Press.

Erickson, T. (2012). The Biggest Mistake You (Probably) Make with Teams. *Harvard Business Review*. Retrieved April 21, 2015, from https://hbr.org/2012/04/the-biggest-mistake-you-probably.

Estrela, A. (2013). *Are You Ready to be Coached?* [Published in the CSTD eNewsletter - November 6, 2013] Retrieved April 25th, 2015, from http://www.shepell.com/pdf/Nov6-2013_AreYouReadyToBeCoached.pdf.

Fink, S. & Markholt, A. (2011). *Leading for Instructional Improvement: How Successful Leaders Develop Teaching and Learning Expertise*. San Francisco: Jossey-Bass.

Fisher, D., Frey, N., & Pumpian, I. (2012). *How to Create a Culture of Achievement in Your School and Classroom*. Alexandria, VA: Association for Supervision and Curriculum Development.

Fletcher, S. & Mullen, C. (2012). *The SAGE Handbook of Mentoring and Coaching in Education*. London: SAGE.

Friend, M., Cook, L., Harley-Chamberlin, D., & Shamberger, C. (2010). Co-teaching: An Illustration of the Complexity of Collaboration in Special Education. *Journal of Educational and Psychological Consultation, 20*: 9–27.

Gallucci, C., DeVoogt Van Lare, M., Yoon, I. H., & Boatright, B. (2010). Instructional Coaching: Building Theory About the Role and Organizational Support for Professional Learning. *American Education Research Journal, 47*: 919. Originally Published Online 9 June 2010, DOI: 10.3102/0002831210371497. Retrieved from https://www.k–12leadership.org/sites/default/files/gallucci_aerj_article.pdf.

Garmston, R. J., & Wellman, B. M. (2013). *The Adaptive School: A Sourcebook for Developing Collaborative Groups,* 2nd edition. Lanham, MD: Rowman & Littlefield, Education Division.

Gerstein, Jackie. The Educator with a Growth Mindset: A Staff Workshop. User Generated Education. August 28, 2014. Accessed July 26, 2015. https://usergeneratededucation.wordpress.com/2014/08/29/the-educator-wit.

Gerstein, J. (2013, June 20). Education 3.0: Altering Round Peg in Round Hole Education [Web Log Post]. Retrieved from https://usergeneratededucation.wordpress.com/2013/06/09/education-3-0-altering-round-peg-in-round-hole-education/.

Glick, M. (2011). *The Instructional Leader and the Brain: Using Neuroscience to Inform Practice*. Thousand Oaks, CA: Corwin Press.

Grissom, J. A., Loeb, S., & Master, B. (2013, October). Effective Instructional Time use for School Leaders: Longitudinal Evidence from Observation of Principals. *Educational Researcher, 42*(8): 433–44.

Hargraves, A. & Fullan, M. (2012). *Professional Capital: Transforming Teaching in Every School*. New York: Teachers College Press.

Harris, S. & Edmondson, S. (2013). *The Trust Factor: Strategies for School Leaders*. New York: Routledge.

Harris, A. S., Bruster, B., Peterson, B., & Shutt, T. (2010). *Examining and Facilitating Reflection to Improve Professional Practice*. Lanham, MD: Rowman & Littlefield, Education Division.

Hattie, J. (2012). *Visible Learning for Teachers: Maximizing Impact on Learning*. New York: Routledge.

Hattie, J. (2009). *Visible Learning: A Synthesis of Over 800 Meta-Analyses Relating to Achievement*. New York: Routledge.

International Literacy Association. (2004). *The Role and Qualifications of the Reading Coach in the United States*. [Position Statement.] Retrieved April 20, 2015, from http://www.reading.org/Libraries/position-statements-and resolutions/ ps1065_reading_coach.pdf

Interstate New Teacher Assessment and Support Consortium. (2013, April). *Model Core Teaching Standards and Learning Progressions for Teachers 1.0*. Washington, DC: Council of Chief State School Officers.

Ippolito, J. (2010). Three Ways that Literacy Coaches Balance Responsive and Directive Relationships with Teachers. *Elementary School Journal, 3:* 164–90.

Johnson, J. (2011). *You Can't Do it Alone: A Communications and Engagement Manual for School Leaders*. Lanham, MD: Rowman & Littlefield Education.

Karcinski, L. J. (2015). *Five School District Mentor Models for Secondary Mathematics and Science Teachers in a Job Embedded University Teacher Preparation Program*. Orlando: University of Central Florida, Unpublished Dissertation.

Kardos, S. M., & Johnson, S. (2010). New Teachers' Experiences of Mentoring: The Good, the Bad, and the Inequity. *Journal of Educational Change, 11*(1): 23–44. Doi: 10.1007/s10833-008-9096-4

Killion, J. & Harrison, C. (2006). *Taking the Lead: New Roles for Teachers and School-Based Coaches*. Oxford, OH: National Staff Development Council.

Knight, J., (Editor). (2009). *Coaching Approaches and Perspectives*. Thousand Oaks, CA. Corwin Press.

Knight, J., Elford, M., Hock, M. Dunekack, K., Bradley, B., Dashler, D. D., & Knight, D. (2015, February). 3 Steps to Great Coaching: A Simple but Powerful Instructional Coaching Cycly Nets Results. *Journal of Staff Development, 36*(1): 11–18.

Lewis, C. C. & Hurd, J. (2011). *Lesson Study Step by Step: How Teacher Learning Communities Improve Instruction*. Portsmouth, NH: Heinemann.

Lewis, C., Perry, R., Foster, D., Hurd, J., & Fisher, L. (2011). Lesson Study: Beyond Coaching. *Educational Leadership, 69*(2): 64–68.

Louis, K. S., Dretzke, B., & Wahlstrom, K. (2010). How Does Leadership Affect Student Achievement? Results from a National Survey. *School Effectiveness and Improvement: An International Journal of Research, Policy, and Practice, 21*(3): 315–36.

Lyons, C., & Pinnell, G. (2001). *Systems for Change in Literacy Education: A Guide to Professional Development.* Portsmouth, NH: Heinemann.

Mangin, M. M. & Dunsmore, K. (2014). How the Framing of Instructional Coaching as a Lever for Systematic or Individual Reform Influences the Enactment of Coaching. *Educational Administration Quarterly, 51*(2): 179–213.

Moxley, D. & Taylor, R. T. (2006). *Literacy Coaching: A Handbook for School Leaders.* Thousand Oaks, CA. Corwin Press; Reston, VA: NASSP.

National Center on Quality Teaching and Learning. (2014). *Practice Based Coaching: Collaborative Partnerships.* Retrieved April 28, 2015, from http://eclkc.ohs.acf.hhs.gov/hslc/tta-system/teaching/docs/what-do-we-know-about-coaching.pdf.

Nettles, S. M., & Herrington, C. (2007). Revisiting the Importance of the Direct Effects of School Leadership on Student Achievement: The Implications for School Improvement Policy. *Peabody Journal of Education, 82*(4): 724–36.

Neufeld, B. & Roper, D. (2003). *Coaching: A Strategy for Developing Instructional Capacity, Promises and Practicalities.* Washington, DC: The Aspen Institute. Retrieved May 2, 2015, from http://www.annenberginstitute.org/publications/reports.html.

Oliver, M. (2009). Listening to the Learners: Mentee's Perspectives of a Mentoring Program for First-Year Science Teachers. *Teaching Science: The Journal of the Australian Science Teachers Association, 55*(4): 6–11.

Osmond, S. J. (2015). *A Case Study of the Two-Semester Job Embedded Internship.* Unpublished Dissertation. Orlando: University of Central Florida.

Pink, D. H. (2011). *Drive: The Surprising Truth About What Motivates Us.* New York: Riverhead Books.

Puig, E. A. & Froelich, K. S. (2011). *The Literacy Coach: Guiding in the Right Direction 2nd edition.* Boston: Allyn & Bacon Publishers.

Robertson, J. (2008). The 3 Rs for Coaching Learning Relationships. *Policy and Practice.* Retrieved May 5, 2015, from http://www.educationalleaders.govt.nz/Leadership-development/Professional-information/Considering-principalship/Mentoring-and-coaching/Coaching-Learning-Relationships.

Robinson, V. M. J., Lloyd, C. A., & Rowe, K. J. (2008). The Impact of Leadership on Student Outcomes: An Analysis of the Differential Effects of Leadership Types. *Educational Administration Quarterly, 44*(5): 635–74.

Russell, J. (n.d.) [Quote] Retrieved April 25, 2015, from http://www.performancedevelopmentservices.com/en/services/coaching/why-should-you-invest-coaching/.

Russell, J. (2011, December 9). Coaching to Success [Web Log Post]. Retrieved from http://www.coachingtosuccess.co.uk/quote/john-russell-managing-director-harley-davidson-europe-ltd/ Managing Director, Harley-Davidson Europe Ltd. (n.d.).

Rutherford, P. (2009). *Why Didn't I Learn this in College.* Alexandria, VA: Just Ask Publications.

Rutherford, P. (2008). *21st Century Mentor's Handbook*: *Creating a Culture of Learning.* Alexandria, VA: Just Ask Publications.

Salavert, R. (2015, January). Coaching: An Apprenticeship Approach for the 21st Century. *International Journal of Educational Leadership and Management, 3*(1): 4–24.

Sanders, W. L. & Rivers, J. C. (1996). *Cumulative and Residual Effects of Teachers on Future Student Achievement.* Knoxville, TE: University of Tennessee.

Saphier, J., Halye-Speca, M. A., & Gower, R. (2008). *The Skillful Teacher: Building Your Teaching Skills.* Acton, MA: Research for Better Teaching, Inc.

Showers, B. & Joyce, B. (1996). The Evolution of Peer Coaching. *Educational Leadership, 53*(6): 12–17.

Sherman, S. & Frea, A. (2004). The Wild West of Executive Coaching. *Harvard Business Review, 82*(11): 82–90.

Speir, C. M. (2015). *The Perceived Effectiveness of Mixed Reality Experience in a Master of Arts in Teaching (MAT) Program for Science, Technology, Engineering, and Mathematics Degreed Individuals.* An Unpublished Dissertation. Orlando: University of Central Florida.

Symonds, K. (2003). *Literacy Coaching: How School Districts can Support a Long-term Strategy in a Short-Term World.* San Francisco: The Bay Area School Reform Collaborative.

Taylor, R. T. (2010). *Leading Learning: Change Student Achievement Today!* Thousand Oaks, CA: Corwin Press.

Taylor, R. T. (2007). *Improving Reading, Writing, and Content Learning.* Thousand Oaks, CA: Corwin Press.

Taylor, R. T. & Gordon, W. R. (2014, June). Partnership in Professional Learning: The East Learning Community High School Reading (ELCHSR) Initiative. *Journal of Staff Development, 35*(3): 16–20.

Taylor, R. T. & Gunter, G. (2006). *The Literacy Leadership Fieldbook.* Thousand Oaks, CA: Corwin Press.

Taylor, R. T. & Moxley, D. E. (2008, Summer). Leadership for Literacy Coaching: Evolving Research. *ERS Spectrum. Educational Research Service, 26*(3): 1–6.

Taylor, R., Moxley, D., Chanter, C., & Boulware, D. (2007). Three Techniques for Successful Literacy Coaching. Retrieved April 26, 2015, from http://www.principals.org/portals/0/content/55194.pdf.

Taylor, R. T. & Shanoff, M. (2015, January). Hitting the Learning Target: How to Facilitate Student Motivation and Resilience. *Principal Leadership, 15*(5): 28–31.

Taylor, R. T. & Watson, R. (2013, October). Raising Rigor for Middle and High School Non-proficient Readers. *Principal Leadership, 14*(2): 56–59. Reston, VA: National Association of Secondary School Principals.

Taylor, R. T., Watson, R., & Nutta, J. (2014, July). *Leading, Teaching, Learning for Success with Common Core State Standards.* Lanham, MD: Rowman & Littlefield Publishers.

Taylor, R. T., Zugelder, B., & Bowman, P. (2013, June). Literacy Coach Effectiveness: The Need for Measurement. *International Journal of Mentoring and Coaching in Education, 2*(1): 34–46.

The Alliance Guide to Being Coached. (n.d.). Retrieved April 26, 2015, from http://
   www.alliancecoaching.co.uk/wp-content/uploads/2014/10/Guide-Being-Coached.
   pdf

Tishman, S. & Perkins, D. N. (1997). The Language of Thinking. *Phi Delta Kappan,*
   78(5): 368–374.

Tishman, S., Perkins, D. N., & Jay, E. (1995). *The Thinking Classroom.* Boston:
   Allyn & Bacon.

Walpole, S., & Blamey, K. (2008). Elementary Literacy Coaches: The Reality of Dual
   Roles. *The Reading Teacher, 62*(3): 222–31.

Washburn-Moses, L. (2010). Rethinking Mentoring: Comparing Policy and Practice
   in Special and General Education. *Education Policy Analysis Archives, 18*(32):
   1–22.

Wenglinsky, H. (2000). *How Teaching Matters: Bringing the Classroom Back Into*
   Discussions of Teacher Quality. Princeton, NJ: Policy Information Center.

Wren, S., & Reed, D. (2005). Literacy Coaches Roles and Responsibilities. Published
   in *SEDL Letter, 17*(1). Reaching Our Reading Goals.

Index

ability, 32, 37, 39
academic language, 56–57, 61
accountability, 14;
    reciprocal, 45, 87, 91
achievement, 18, 27, 31, 35, 38–39, 45,
    56, 59, 70, 82, 95, 97
active listening, 53–54, 62
The Adaptive School (Garmston &
    Wellman), 71
administrators:
    coaching partnership role of, 23–25;
    and content, 11;
    and continually improve expertise
        practice, 90;
    and curriculum, 11;
    and effective adult communication
        practice, 61;
    and engagement, 12;
    generative thinking, 31–39;
    and learning environment, 11;
    and pedagogy, 11–12;
    tips for, 28, 38–39, 47–48, 59–60,
        72–73, 89, 99–100
adult learning, 18, 24, 63, 74
Aguilar, Elena, 22
AmeriCorps, 78
The Annenberg Institute, 18, 23
Art of Coaching Teachers, 22

Association of Supervision and
    Curriculum Development
    (ASCD), 24

body and mind alignment, in adult
    communication, 53

capacity-building progress, 25, 30,
    77–78, 82, 87, 99
case study:
    coaching and mentoring, 3–4;
    coaching partnership process, 68–70;
    coaching partnership relationship,
        45–46;
    coaching partnership roles, 25–27;
    commitment to empowerment,
        94–96;
    continual development of expertise,
        86–87;
    e-mail communication, 57;
    generative thinking, 35–37
The Center for Educational Leadership
    at the University of Washington,
    97
closed-thinking disposition, 33
coach and mentor:
    coaching partnership role of, 21–23;
    and content, 9;

Harley-Davidson Europe Ltd., 73
Hattie, John, 8, 78
high-effect size strategies, 7
high-impact strategies, 7

ILA. *See* International Literacy
    Association (ILA)
*Improving Reading, Writing, and
    Content Learning* (Taylor), 78
individual coaching, 64–65
in-person meetings, 44
inquiry-based coaching process, 8, 9,
    14, 21, 31–34, 38, 43–46, 53, 55,
    56, 64, 71–72, 74
inquiry-driven learning, 87
Inside Mathematics (http://
    insidemathematics.org), 13
instructional differentiation, 84–85
The Instructional Leader and the Brain
    (Glick), 86
instructional planning, 84–85
instructional rounds or walkthroughs,
    85–86
InTASC. *See* Interstate Teacher
    Assessment and Support
    Consortium (InTASC) Model
International Literacy Association
    (ILA), 17
Interstate Teacher Assessment and
    Support Consortium (InTASC)
    Model, 72
INVEST video series, 10, 13

job-embedded:
    coaching process, 63, 66, 74;
    professional learning, 1, 21, 98

Kansas University Center for Research
    on Learning: Instructional
    Coaching video archive, 25
Knight, Jim, 25, 68

large-scale coaching and mentoring, 66
leaders, and sustainable change,
    96–97

*Leading, Teaching, Learning the
    Common Core Standards* (Taylor,
    Watson, & Nutta), 8, 10, 78
learner:
    coaching partnership role of,
        19–20;
    and content knowledge, 6;
    and continually improve expertise
        practice, 89;
    and curriculum, 6–7;
    and effective adult communication
        practice, 60;
    and engagement, 8;
    generative thinking, 31–39;
    and learning environment, 5;
    and pedagogy, 7–8;
    tips for, 27, 37–38, 47, 57–58, 71,
        88, 97–98
learning:
    collaborative, 10, 11;
    inquiry-driven, 87;
    job-embedded, 1, 21, 98
learning environment:
    and administrators, 11;
    and coach and mentor, 9;
    and learner, 5
lesson study, 81
Literacy Coaching (Moxley &
    Taylor), 10
Literacy Coaching Clearing House,
    20, 23
Literacy System, 95–96
Little Red School House Award, 82
Lucas Education Research, 89

Mathematics Coaching, K–12
    (Bay-Williams & McGatha), 10
metacognition/thinking, 2, 12, 27, 30,
    31, 37, 48, 52, 56, 73
mistake making, and risk-taking, 38
modeling, and relationship building,
    42–43
model reciprocal accountability, 90

novice teachers, 5, 7, 22, 30, 58, 86, 88

About the Authors

Rosemarye (Rose) Taylor is professor of educational leadership at the University of Central Florida (UCF). Her specialty is systematic leadership to improve student achievement Pk–20, particularly with improved literacy. She collaborates across disciplines and borders to improve student learning and effectiveness of professionals in education and education-related industry. To cite an example, she is part of an ERASMUS-funded international research on supervising doctoral students and programs.

She has received numerous awards. Most recently, she has received the UCF Doctoral Student Mentoring Award, and was honored as one of the UCF Women Making History. Also, Oak Ridge High School honored her as an inductee in the Alumni Hall of Fame for her contributions to her own high school's systematic processes for learning. Recent professional volunteerism includes: serving as President of the Florida Association of Professors of Educational Leadership, being a member of the Executive Board of the Florida Association of School Administrators, and serving as Editor of the *International Journal of Educational Leadership Preparation.*

Prior to joining the educational leadership faculty at UCF, Dr. Taylor was national director of professional development for Scholastic Inc. She has served as a school-based and school district administrator in Florida and Georgia. Through instructional leadership in schools, school districts, and at UCF, along with being the director for the Orange County Literacy Project which served as the model for the development of *Read 180*, her work has touched the lives of thousands.

She has published articles in *Kappan, Educational Leadership, Middle School Journal, Schools in the Middle, American Secondary Education, AASA Professor, The National Staff Development Journal, Principal Leadership, The School Administrator, Educational Research Service Spectrum,*

International Journal of Mentoring and Coaching in Education, AASA Journal of Scholarship and Practice, and *International Journal of Education Management.* Also, she has authored seven books, the most recent of which are:

Taylor, R. T., Watson, R., & Nutta, J. (July 2014). *Leading, teaching, learning for success with common core state standards.* Lanham, MD: Rowman & Littlefield Publishers.

Taylor, R. T. (2010). *Leading learning: Change student achievement today!* Thousand Oaks, CA: Corwin Press.

Dr. Carol Chanter has more than thirty years of experience in the K–12 setting as a special and general educator as well as a school and district administrator. During the past nine years she has utilized this experience in her roles as vice president, Implementation Services for Scholastic Achievement Partners and most recently as senior vice president, Program Professional Services at Houghton Mifflin Harcourt to liaise with school and district leaders regarding best practices in program implementation, literacy intervention, high-leverage instructional practices, and school turnaround.

Dr. Chanter believes that there are five key mechanisms for improving student learning: learning environments that offer a sense of respect and belonging, a teaching culture that values content knowledge, a standards-based curriculum, effective pedagogical practices, and cognitively engaging learning tasks.

She has presented at numerous conferences and has authored and coauthored several articles. Her areas of interest and expertise include general and special education, educational leadership, and K–12 literacy. She has taught courses at the University of Central Florida in organization and administration of schools, contemporary issues in education, management of reading programs, and secondary reading.

Carol received her bachelor of arts degree in Education from the University of Florida, her master's degree in learning and behavior disorders from the University of Kentucky, her education specialist degree in educational leadership from Nova University, and her doctorate in educational research, technology, and leadership from the University of Central Florida.

Lo que le encanta a Conejito

Por Cyndy Szekeres
Traducido por Alberto Téllez Aguilar
a través de Editorial Trillas, S.A. de C.V.

A Golden Book • New York
Western Publishing Company, Inc., Racine, Wisconsin 53404

Este es Conejito.

Esto es lo que le encanta.

Conejito ama a Mamá.

Conejito ama a Papi.

A Conejito le encanta el bebé.

Conejito se divierte con él.

A Conejito le encanta correr.

Corre alrededor de un árbol.

Le encanta hacer pasteles.

¡Le encanta comer pasteles!

A Conejito le encanta jugar.

Juega con su amigo.

Juega con un carrito.

Juega con una gran pelota.

A Conejito le encanta ponerse
sombrerotes y sombreritos.

Le encanta andar en triciclo.

A Conejito le encanta trabajar.

Le encanta hacer cosas.

A Conejito le encantan todas
las cosas buenas para comer.

Le encanta ayudar a su Papi.

A Conejito le encanta leer.

A Conejito le encanta pintar.

A Conejito le encanta su barco.

¡Le encanta montar sobre su Papi...,

... hasta llegar a la cama!

¡Buenas noches, Conejito!